What people are sa about Steve Abel

"I met Steve at a 4N meeting where he gave a truly inspiring talk on the personal motivation needed to build a multimillion pound company. It was the best 4Sight I have seen in 3½ years at 4N; and he had me really believing I COULD do it!" – Geoff Baldwin

"I filmed Steve speaking at the Bedfordshire Business Women Network in April 2012. I have to say I thought his presentation was extremely inspiring and would be of interest to anyone thinking of starting out in business."

– Mario Crispino, Video Production Specialist, AVI Works

"Steve delivered an interesting and well received seminar at one of our regional Business Growth Shows. He managed to balance content with an enthusiasm that was appreciated by our audience of business leaders." – John Plaster

"I heard Steve speak at a networking meeting last week and he was fantastic. The story he has to tell about his life is truly inspirational and an example to all budding business people. He encapsulates the saying 'the only limits you have are the ones you place on yourselves'. If you get the opportunity to hear him then you shouldn't hesitate to do so." – Howard Schaverien MIFS DipFA

"A genuinely inspirational story for anybody in business already, or just starting out ..... he has the ability to connect with his audience, motivate, and to really demonstrate the qualities, skills and determination required in order to succeed. Very highly recommended." – Simon Taylor

"Steve is a local hero here in Banbury. When he gave a talk to our Young Enterprise students, they were rivited. He is inspiring, and is one of those people in life who seem to attract good luck. There are some who say you make your own luck, in which case, look out for Stephen, he is going places." – Sue Priest, Verifi, LLC

"His passion and drive comes across in bucket loads, and his delivery is further enhanced by the honesty through which he talks. His style is not polished, corporate and cold - it is open, from the heart and therefore totally accessible to anyone in business. It's a message of can-do with powerful energy to back it up. He makes you remember why you started in business in the first place and makes you realise that you can have that passion again, never mind how long you've been doing it!" – Nick Haine, Aitch Em

"I was priviliged to hear Steve speak at a recent 4N meeting. His frankness, humility and accounts of his experiences were woven into his presentation which he delivered in a relaxed an personable manner. The presentation oozed authenticity, and really made me think about how I approach challenges. I also came away feeling encouraged to think more positively about challenges and risks. Really well done." – Phil Heard

"Steve's raw honesty about himself, mixed with a powerful message and charismatic presence made for a great start to a cold Wednesday morning. I think that every person in the room was fired up afterwards, inspired to 'wow' their clients that day and beyond! Steve and I hit it off immediately in our subsequent one to one and I instinctively referred him to a friend of mine who would benefit from his services - to the tune of £20-30k a year in fact! It's not very often you meet someone with real presence and with so many business miles under his belt already and plenty of gas left in the tank. I think that this is just the beginning for Steve Abel."

— Stuart Warwick, Business Growth Specialist

SUNMAKERS

HOW TO START SMALL TO BUILD A £MILLION BUSINESS THAT WILL RUN WITHOUT YOU

BIG FISH LITTLE FISH

Steve Abel

SUNMAKERS

BIG FISH LITTLE FISH
HOW TO START SMALL TO BUILD A £MILLION BUSINESS THAT WILL RUN WITHOUT YOU

Published by Sunmakers, a division of Eldamar Ltd,
157 Oxford Road, Cowley, Oxford, OX4 2ES, UK
www.sunmakers.co.uk
Tel +44(0)1865 779944

First Edition

Designed by Ayd Instone, www.sunmakers.co.uk

978-1-908693-07-5

www.steveabel.co.uk

To all entrepreneurs who are serious about taking their business to the next level.

Acknowledgements

There are plenty of folk without whose help I wouldn't be where I am today. Specifically, my thanks go to:

Mum and dad, Sally and David Abel - thanks for encouraging me in everything I do. And thanks, dad, for helping and directing me in the early days of business.

Roberta – for living with me when I am focused on a project; it's not an easy thing to do. I'm an all or nothing kind of guy, working day and night on a project at the expense of everything else. My apologies for neglecting you while I was writing this book. I'd also like to say a big thank you for coming up with the name for this book; after hearing me talk about my fish analogy far too many times.

My daughters, Jasmine and Sophie - although I don't see you as much as I'd like to, you're always with me in my thoughts. Looking forward to hanging out with you when you're older, preferably on exotic holidays and doing lots of fun stuff.

My editor, Chris Bown – thanks for helping with ordering my thoughts and turning them into properly spelt, grammatically correct English in this, my first book.

Ayd Instone and Sunmakers for making the book look good and come to life.

Creating Media for doing the freehand illustrations in the book and for also creating my website www.steveabel.co.uk

Then there's the P4D team, who have helped me create my best business yet:

Kerrie - my first ever employee, who knows the business inside out. She joined me as a data entry clerk and now manages our customer support. Thanks for putting in more than most would, when the business really needed it.

Amanda - a customer service guru, fluent in the language of international import and export. An animal lover, we adopted Amanda a donkey and a Shetland pony.

Chris – our chief geek, Chris has been in web development a long time, and transformed the P4D booking operation in to an award-winning system.

Colin – known as The Major, he keeps the troops in order. He not only served in the army, but is a trained nurse, so he's our resident medic too.

Jonathon - our credit controller and business analyst, who also dons the blue lycra suit to be our P4D Superhero!

Natalie - responsible for brand and communications. A furious networker and social butterfly, she sends out our message to the masses.

Rob - our business development guru, Rob can find you last minute space on a plane or a fair price on an unusual shipment. He's also our top bowler!

Julie - as our claims manager, Julie makes the resolution process as stress free as possible for everyone, picking up valuable feedback on the way.

Trevor – who's travelled most of the world and knows the exact location of most destinations. Specialist subject: pallet deliveries.

Lisa - as the mum of three lovely girls, Lisa comes to work for a rest. Answering customers' emails and phone calls, she is passionate about getting things right.

Tracey - we know how vital it is to have a great cake maker on the team! Once a cruise ship hairstylist, today she ensures customers are delighted.

Terry - when he's not moonlighting as a Patrick Stewart lookalike, Terry looks after our local customers. He's captain of his own ship, flying in and out of the office.

Laura – between stints helping the customer service team, Laura studies fashion, and is always in vogue.

Lauren - a long distance runner, Lauren helps out in the holidays, racing high, low and cross country to help our customers reach the finish line.

Jodie – our resident redhead, Jodie mixes shifts at P4D with studying financial maths at university – it's not her temper that's fiery, it's her brain!

Janice - first to pick up the phone and quick to assign enquiries to the right department, Janice is a mad film buff – lights, camera, action!

Sophie - our secret agent, she always has every angle covered. She is also a painter, book lover and food enthusiast, with a voice that sounds like caramel.

Petrina – No longer with us, as she left to raise her family, she's sorely missed and was a key player in growing the company.

Pippa - multi-talented Pippa has worked for a radio station, and also used to breed and show dogs. She can drive a tractor, and a bus... why? Nobody knows!

Without all of you guys, the business would not be where it is today. You guys rock! Thank you!

Contents

Foreword

What helps define success? Plenty of management books have been written encouraging us to "double your rate of failure", instructing "don't sweat the small stuff" and "just do it".

Now, here's a fresh collection of ideas, assembled by a young entrepreneur with a real world story thrashed out in the English provinces. It's not a rags to riches story, nor the tale of someone who had a lucky break, or who started with a silver spoon in his mouth. He was blessed by a supportive family though, as he notes, those who love you most cannot always be guaranteed to understand the entrepreneurial mindset.

From those early schoolboy shifts washing cars, Steve Abel clearly had an entrepreneurial streak, but his first eight businesses were – as he's happy to now admit – nothing special. Most of them had a moment or two of success in a crowded market, before succumbing to changing circumstances, or tougher competition.

But their great value, learned from the ups and downs he candidly shares, was in the lessons learnt when he spotted his truly innovative business opportunity, Parcels 4 Delivery. With P4D, he harnessed the power of group buying, and the magic of internet technology – something he himself had once dismissed as time-wasting "geekery". He finally built a business on solid foundations, with massive growth potential. And along the way, he discovered how to grow something that's much more than simply self-employment; rather a sustainable business that employs a growing, capable team; with systems that mean its success is no longer dependent on him working all hours.

Business success has not come without cost. His drive and passion for business have caused some casualties along the way, in his personal life. And he put in the time and effort, when many would have given up.

Is that the end of the tale? It's probably best to think of it as the first chapter in what may well turn out to be an even more interesting story. Steve is now devoting a portion of his time to encouraging, mentoring and supporting others to find their own success, by sharing his experiences.

This book is arranged in two parts. The first takes you through Steve's story, as he created new businesses, developed and grew through his experiences to date. The second extracts some of the techniques and skills he learnt and has successfully employed, and shares them with you. They worked for Steve, you may find them beneficial.

Chris Bown, Editor
February 2013

Part One

Introduction

I've been very sceptical about writing a book, but I am constantly being prompted to write one by friends and business associates. I guess it's because I have achieved a reasonably high level of success in a short period of time. Without many qualifications but with a passion and determination to succeed, I am now proud to say I have a multi million pound business based in the growing town of Banbury, Oxfordshire. As I write this, it currently employs eighteen staff.

It hasn't all been easy, I've had nine companies in total. All of them were successful, however eight of them only provided me with a lifestyle income; they basically paid the bills but I knew none of them were going to be scalable. It wasn't until 2005 I had my "light bulb" moment; I stumbled across yet another business idea, but I knew straight away this was a business that had a multi million pound potential.

By the way, even at this stage of my life in 2005 aged 29 years of age, I still didn't label myself as an entrepreneur. In my eyes I was someone who was self employed, I was my own boss and I had already proved to myself I could earn more money than most of my friends at my age who were working in the corporate world. One of my weaknesses is materialistic items, cars, holidays, and nice clothes and I'll admit I lived beyond my means - in other words, I know what it's like to be in lots of debt to credit card companies.

So, getting back to my light bulb moment. I left school in 1991, and then did a year at college doing a business diploma. I was straight into my first business aged 16 selling reconditioned televisions. The next business was selling reconditioned washing machines and fridge-freezers. I'll digress later in the book about each business, but for now I want to quickly list them here so you can get a quick picture of my business career so far. My third business was a domestic appliance training school. Forth company was an export business. Fifth business was importing jeans from USA. Sixth business was in property. Seventh business was being a professional horse racing tipster. Eighth business was selling mini motorbikes. All these businesses I have listed were "lifestyle" businesses; when I couldn't work due to holidays or ill health, they were not making money.

I think we can agree starting and running lifestyle businesses is something that doesn't scare me. I'd find it more daunting if I had to go and get a job working for another company. My comfort zone is very different to the norm, and I found it strange when friends said they found me inspiring; other entrepreneurs who are reading this will relate to this. All that said, I was now at a new cross roads in my life where I had just had my light bulb moment, an idea that actually scared me, not because it was a new idea, but because I knew it had that multi million pound potential and I knew I wasn't the man for the job. Why would I believe I could set up a big successful company? I have no previous experience in running a million pound turnover business - so it was all too easy to dismiss the whole idea. I had to change my mindset, I had to find a way to believe I could do this and I'll divulge my secrets later.

1: Pocket money talks

So where shall I start? So you can get a really good understanding of what makes me tick, I'm going to go right back to my childhood. I also find when we go over our past and take a close look at it, we learn more about ourselves as we're kind of looking at it through an older pair of eyes.

I'm the youngest of three, the baby, and I say this because I remember being referred to as the baby, albeit I am the biggest, weighing in at 16 and a half stone and 6ft 4inches. My brother Sean was the oldest, four years my senior and then my sister Jackie, two years my senior, the apple of my dad's eye. I completely get it now, now I have two daughters myself, who are both the apple of their dad's eye.

Rather than going right through my childhood, I'll keep this business orientated. If my mum was writing this she would tell you: "At the end of Stephen's first week of primary school, I was standing at the school gates with all the other mothers waiting for our children to come out. Stephen came out with his coat hanging off one shoulder and his bag over the other. One of the other mothers asked Stephen 'Did you have a nice day?' and he replied 'No! It's a complete waste of my time, the school's time and the teachers' time and I really can't see the point of it all'. I was shocked at his response." I don't remember this but my mum takes the opportunity to embarrass me with this story whenever she gets the opportunity. Mums are good at doing this, but I love her for it.

It sounds daft and I'm ashamed to admit it, but It took me a while to figure out why we need to go to school, so I didn't really apply myself until I was in the third year (year 9) after being sat down by my parents and being given a wake up call. My dad reached the point where he didn't enjoy attending parent's evening. My mum and dad used to hear the same thing year after year: "Stephen is behind a locked door, and we are yet to find the key." Little did they know their little boy was destined to be a serial entrepreneur, and would go on to be the founder of a successful multi million pound company within the next 15 years.

I managed to finish my schooling with a couple of GCSE grade Cs, but the rest were embarrassingly low grades.

The truth is, my true entrepreneurial flare first revealed itself when I was 14. My mum and dad taught me about the value of money and encouraged me to wash cars in the street for a pound or two. I remember taking a lot of pride in washing cars, once I had started applying that soapy sponge to the dirty car and seeing the shiny paint work shine through, I had a feeling of pride come over me and I had to clean it as best I could. I wouldn't say I actually enjoyed washing cars, it was hard work but I wasn't the sort to do a shoddy job and leave a car with streaks on it where I hadn't rinsed it off or leathered it properly. I think in my head I really enjoyed seeing the reactions from the owners of the vehicles and hearing comments like: "It hasn't looked that clean since it was new", or: "I can see my reflection in it." The £1 or £2 charge usually ended up being a couple of quid more in the way of a tip because of the attention to detail I used to put in, but I never asked for more.

I suppose the subconscious, clever bit at the time is the way I won more customers to wash and clean cars for; my dad is a reverend and was the minister at the local church in the village of Deddington. I attended church every Sunday morning with my family, and as you can imagine there were a fair few people there who had cars. Some of the old folk I was already washing cars for were members of the church, and as crazy as it sounds, I was getting good introductions and recommendations as this lovely young man, son of the minister who did a really good job of washing cars. Was this a business? No of course not, but it was a 14 year old boy learning about some of the core values of a strong business.

If I think back even before this, my sister Jackie had a paper round, delivering the local free paper to all the houses in the village. I don't know how old I was, but I do remember I was too young to get the job directly with the newsagent, but my sister needed help, so we agreed on a split of the money she got paid. I think I got one or two pounds out of the £5 she received. I remember I didn't have a money box, and I used to use one of the drawers of a small chocolate truffle box which my mum and dad use to have in the lounge. Over the weeks and months of helping with my sister's paper round and washing cars in the village, I remember seeing that little drawer accumulate a lot of £1 and 50p coins.

I remember being really good at not spending too much of it on sweets because I had this particular thing I was saving to buy. I already had a classical nylon string guitar but I really wanted a particular black electric guitar which was on display in the local music shop in Banbury - it cost about £129, I think. I remember walking in the shop with a small wedge of notes (I had got the £1 coins changed) and buying that guitar. I had all my family with me and it was quite a proud moment.

Was this the key point in my life that triggered off the entrepreneur in me? No, I'm not saying by saving my pennies and buying a guitar, but by learning about the core values behind all of this. In my opinion you can't just be taught this, you have to learn about this by actually doing it. I had nothing to start with, apart from 50p pocket money each week and a bucket and sponge. Kids today have it too easy, and all we're doing is making it harder for them when they're adults.

There is also another little business I got involved in when I was 14 or 15, but very few people know about it and I am sceptical about mentioning it in here. Not even my parents know about it - but don't worry, it wasn't drugs. I'm not massively proud of it, but looking back I can now identify the entrepreneurial mind at work. If you want to know what is was, you'll have to read on as some readers might find it shocking and stop reading now. Ah stuff it, I'll tell you now otherwise if I say it at the end, it'll be the last thing you remember about me and if you read it now, you'll hopefully forget about it. My very first part time employed Saturday job was in Acorn stores, a village grocery store, stacking shelves and occasionally operating the cash register. I ended up getting fired because I didn't rotate the mushrooms when the manager asked me.

The actual truth of this was, it was one of those times when someone asks you to do something and you didn't hear them properly, so I applied the three times rule, it's where you say pardon three times and after the third time, if you still didn't understand them, you just nod your head and say yes and pretend you heard them. Looking back, I wish I had spoken up and said: "Speak properly and mouth your words so I can understand you" (haha), but I was just a kid and I was raised to respect my elders. I went straight from Acorn Stores, along the way to the local newsagents and post office, where I landed myself a job behind the counter on a Saturday, and Thursday and Friday evening after school. After working here for a few months I had learnt the ropes from running the video library, keeping the sweets stocked up and making sure the newspapers and magazines were constantly updated and rotated. Oh boy, I can't believe I'm going to tell you this. Well, all of the top shelf magazines were the naughty magazines, which could only be sold to over 18's. Every week I had to go through all the magazines making sure there were no old copies and everything was up to date. When new batches of magazines came in, the old copies were taken out the back and stacked in an alleyway out the back for recycling, including the naughty rude ones like Mayfair,

Penthouse and so on. After work I use to walk around the back of the shop and take a few copies, the following day I would sneak them into school and sell them in the school playground for twice as much as the cover price.

Is this stealing? I don't think so; they were all stored in an area by the wheelie bins which anyone could access. I think it's worse that I was the vicar's son, hence why it was kept very quiet. Could you imagine if I had got caught? Suspension, expulsion, or even worse, local news headlines: "Vicar's son, 15, expelled for selling porn in school". There I've said it, I just hope you can forgive me and appreciate the entrepreneurialism in this, instead of the filth I was selling at the age of 15.

2: Tough love

So I'm 16 years old and living with my parents. I'm at college five days a week and holding down a part time job behind the deli counter at Tesco. Four hours on a Thursday and Friday evening, and eight hours on a Saturday. I couldn't sustain this for anything longer than about eight months, but it was giving me a bit of extra pocket money to spend on clothes and housekeeping, yes housekeeping. My mum and dad were pretty strict, and looking back on it, it was for our own good, actually maybe this could be a big contributor to the success my life has become.

I said our mum and dad were very strict, actually it's more like my dad was very strict and my mum would support him. I eventually found ways to play my mum and get her round my little finger, but boy would I get it when my dad got home from work and when I say get it, we're not talking just a little talking to. However, I respected my dad a great deal, but maybe I was a little scared of the big fella in the early days before I reached 16.

Mum and dad have some old fashioned morals, and these have passed down to me. One in particular is that they don't agree with a son or daughter living at home with their parents, once they pass a certain age. No actual age was ever specified, but their point was, you're an adult at 18 by which time you should have aspirations for your future and plans to build your own life. Seems harsh, eh! But how does the old adage go? "Be cruel to be kind."

> *We see all too much of these young adults who find it too easy to stay living with their parents right into their late twenties and some into their thirties. Their parents think they're being good to their children, when really they're just making the journey we call life a lot harder.*

So in a nutshell I was going to be on the street if I didn't get my shit together! No, not at all, but I saw what my brother had to put up with so I knew what I had in store. They just made it very difficult for him to stay at home, which fueled him to do whatever it took to pull his finger out and start his life. All three of us are very independent individuals, and don't need to lean on our parents for support; that must be a great and proud feeling for any parent.

Another quick story about my dad, he used to be a driving instructor back in the 70's and early 80's. So when it came to teaching the three of us how to drive, he didn't just teach us around the country lanes of Oxfordshire, he made us drive into central London and navigate through some of the most difficult traffic situations we have ever encountered. I think all three of us were reduced to tears with the pressure, but his thinking behind this is that if we can drive around central London, we can be confident driving almost anywhere. We all passed first time. Enough said, my old man is pretty awesome really.

I may have rambled on about my parents, but I was trying to say whist I was 16, at college and working at Tesco, I was asking myself some really important questions, including: "What is it I want to do for a full time job?" I didn't know, so I asked myself: "What is it that I *don't* want to do for a full time job?" and the list was endless. I knew £12,000 a year income was about the best salary out there for someone my age and with my qualifications (don't forget this was 1991/92). I was beginning to get pretty depressed about all of this, like most lads my age I had a love for fast cars and bikes and I knew £12,000 a year wasn't going to fund a Porsche or a Ferrari any time soon and the thought of climbing a corporate ladder and eventually enjoying a great income when I'm in my 40s/50s, well I just don't have the patience.

My parents lived on a road in Banbury called Bloxham Road. The locals called this road "Millionaires Row". Now please don't think I had an easy start and had really rich parents who lived in a mansion who helped finance my first business, as this would be incorrect. As you leave Banbury on the Bloxham Road, all the houses on the right are £1 million plus houses and all the houses on the left are modest 3/4 bed houses - and we lived on the left side. They were still lovely houses, but not quite like the ones on the other side of the road. My bedroom looked out over some of the properties on the other side of the road.

On weekdays there would be Jaguars, Bentleys and big BMWs running in and out of the drives of these amazing properties, then at the weekend you'd see the toys come out; Porsches, Ferraris, one of them had a beautiful red Ducati motorbike. The house directly opposite had their own gardeners, and the lawns always looked immaculate. I was getting an idea of how much all of this must cost, and the kind of income required to live in a place like this with all the added luxuries and holidays to go with it.

I asked the question that Lloyd Grossman became famous for asking: "Who lives in a house like this?" I was getting mixed answers from different people, but all alluded to big earners. Bank managers, solicitors, barristers, judges, CEOs of big companies but then I heard this peculiar word "entrepreneur". Here I was, 16 years old and this was the first time I had heard the name entrepreneur. What's one of those? The Oxford English dictionary quotes: "The owner or manager of a business enterprise who, by risk and initiative, attempts to make profits." So basically buying and selling and making sure there is a profit to be had, plus I can choose whatever business I want to be in. Cool, I can't see myself getting bored doing something like this.

So with a bit of guidance from my dad, who has quite a bit of entrepreneurial flair himself, we set up my first company: Eye View TVs.

3: The big screen beckons

My dad and I bought a copy of the Exchange & Mart. I think it is still sold today in newsagents. You can buy and sell almost anything in the Exchange & Mart, from kettles and toasters to cars and caravans, but there was also a section on business ideas, from little scams right through to buying complete businesses. It was here we discovered we could buy reconditioned TV's for about £50. I know exactly what you're thinking: "Rodney, this time next year, we're going to be millionaires." I agree it does sound a bit like Del Boy and Rodney from *Only Fools and Horses*, and there were some sceptics in the family that referred to this later on in my career. What they didn't realise is that comments like that just make me more determined.

So instead of trading out of a high rise flat, like Del Boy and Rodney, at aged 17 I took on a shop with a flat above it, on the Warwick Road in Banbury. I stayed living with my parents but later on my older brother Sean took residence of the flat. It was one of about four or five shops in a parade, right on a busy junction in the town. We spent about £50 on materials so we could build strong shelving to sit the TVs on. Remember back to the early 90s, flat screens weren't really around and the TVs we were dealing with were those big heavy ones in wooden cabinets, so the shelving had to be tough and strong. We stocked up all the shelves and we must have sold out every week. For months, we were constantly running back and forth from the supplier in Coventry and Birmingham to collect more TVs to keep the shelves stocked.

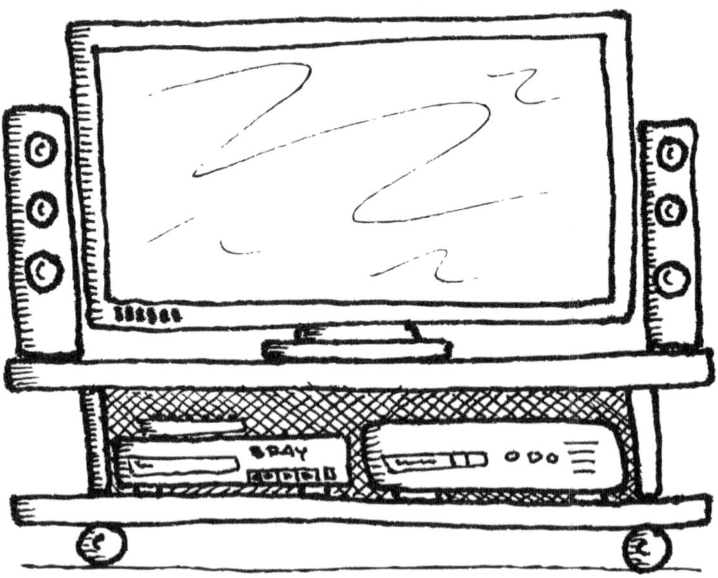

So this is how the finances worked out. We were buying TVs in at cost for between £50 and £100 each, depending on the age and size of the screen, and whether or not it was remote control, as remote controls were quite a luxury back then. My typical selling prices started from £89 and went up to £175 for something a little bit special. We had some TVs that we could ask over £200.00 for, but these were out of the ordinary. After the first few months we came across our first real problem, we had TVs breaking down. This is where I learnt one of my biggest lessons in business, I'll say it now and come back to it.

> *When something poses as a threat to your business, don't back off and surrender to it. Step up and apply yourself and you'll come through it stronger than you were before it happened.*

So here we were making loads of cash, not setting the world aflame but we were building something pretty good. The TVs we were buying came with a three month guarantee, so if it breaks down we're covered - not a problem, you'd think! But the TVs were purchased from warehouses in Birmingham and Coventry, and we were only doing runs once a week to the suppliers. The suppliers wouldn't come all the way over to

Banbury to repair the TVs, while the customers wanted their TVs fixing yesterday.

Well we weren't rogue traders, and I wanted to get things sorted for our valued customers asap because good happy customers refer you to more good happy customers. If they couldn't wait a week, it was a case of replacing the TV or refunding it without a quibble. This just wouldn't do, so we employed our first member of staff who was an ex-Rumbelows TV engineer. Do you remember Rumbelows? We were now in a position where we could repair our faulty TVs quickly.

But instead of buying them reconditioned with three month warranties, we started buying them faulty, and reconditioning them ourselves. This meant our costs had gone from between £50 and £100, down to between £5 and £10. Parts required to recondition each TV were anything from pennies to no more than £10. It wasn't long before we had two TV engineers and a video recorder engineer working for us. So going back to my point, a hurdle that posed itself as an inconvenience in the business actually ended up being an opportunity for a solution that made us more profitable.

You'll notice as I cover more of my business ventures in this book, I'll talk about obstacles, which miraculously turn into opportunities. Some entrepreneurs reading this are nodding their head right now, because you know exactly what I am talking about. I'm now at the stage where an obstacle is welcomed because I have so much experience turning them into opportunities where even more money is made. If everything was plain sailing all the time, firstly it would be boring but secondly, us entrepreneurs would have limited opportunities.

4: When you need to adapt

As a young sales person aged 17, looking back I definitely had some natural sales talent for sure. I call it emotional intelligence and I'll touch more on this later in the book too. Back then, I was using this subconsciously, and it just needed fine-tuning so I could close sales quickly and effectively, instead of taking 30 minutes to eventually get the customer to agree.

I went on a sales course in Rugby, the school was called Key Turn Training I think, this was a real help, teaching me the art of sales, asking open questions, mirroring the customer and then closing the sale without it being too obvious. Call me odd, but I just love being sold to. I was in the room when Brad

Burton, founder and director of 4Networking, and author of *Get Off Your Arse*, asked a room of people: "Who likes to be sold to?" and I was the only one out of about 50 people who stuck my hand up. I felt a bit silly.

Brad was making a valid point about creating the conditions for people to buy, and hard selling can be quite alienating to some potential buyers. I completely agree with Brad on this one; generally, most people don't like being sold to, and that's down to the way the seller approaches the transaction with the wrong mindset, and using the wrong language. Me, I love a good hard sell, but prepare to be critiqued if you're selling to me, or occasionally I'll praise a good sales patter. I really appreciate a good sales pitch.

I'm not good with dates but I'm going to hazard a guess it's about 1994 and we've now expanded into a 2,000 square foot industrial unit, and we still have the small shop with the flat above it on the Warwick Road. By this stage we had four engineers and my dad and I managed to get Sean to join the family business so there were three managers and four staff.

I hardly remember working with Sean, he was only with us for a short time. He left home at 18/19 and had a good job working in sales for a well known corporate firm so it was hard to convince him to join the family business initially, but

I think the pressure got the better of him eventually, plus Eye View TVs was doing so well, we were all convinced we were going to be millionaires. It sounds a bit too good to be true but I can still remember the excitement at the time.

By this time we were also supplying the trade too, so we were selling 10 TVs in bulk for £50 each, so we were now the suppliers. What we failed to predict was about six months down the road; new TVs were getting cheaper in the main high street shops, making secondhand-reconditioned ones less attractive. On top of this we found ourselves competing against Asian businesses that cut their profit margins ruthlessly, which we could not compete with. Our sales were plummeting. Our costs were high now with two properties leased. We had to let three of our staff go, leaving us with one engineer. We had to find a way to increase business again, but based on the fact new TVs in the high street were getting cheaper, it was sensible to accept this was a dying business. Sean made the decision to leave the business and has never looked back, he is high up the corporate ladder for a very well known company.

So we had a good think and I remembered back to something significant from my sales course the year before; it's easier to sell something which people need, instead of something that people want. I suppose a television to some people is classed as a need, but there are other things which come higher on the list of priorities when buying stuff for the house, things like washing machines and fridge freezers. We all need clean clothes and a fridge for the fresh groceries we buy. So the new business was launched.

5:

In a spin

Still going under the trading name of Eye View TVs to begin with, we applied the same business discipline to washing machines, as we had with the TVs. We bought them reconditioned for around £50 to £75, and sold them for between £99 and £150. After a few short months, we realised this was the way forward. We eventually stopped selling TVs and concentrated on washing machines and the occasional fridge freezer.

We were being faced with the same problems as before, washing machines were breaking down and we didn't know how to fix them, and this time it was even more of an inconvenience to swap them over. When you bought a washing machine from me, I'd deliver and install it too. Instead of employing domestic appliance engineers, my dad and I went on a washing machine repair course and after a week or so we knew everything there was to know about Hotpoint and Zanussi washine machines. So why buy them reconditioned when you can buy them broken for £10?

You're probably wondering where do you buy broken washing machines? No, I did not go down to the local council recycling centre. When you buy a new washing machine from leading stores such as Currys, you are given the option for the delivery driver to take away your old washing machine. Where does your old washing machine go to? Well I knew of one place in Aylesbury, Buckinghamshire. But you couldn't just turn up and take what you wanted. A company called Unique Appliances in Coventry had won the contract with the warehouse in Aylesbury, and the deal was you had to take everything each week and take all their cardboard too.

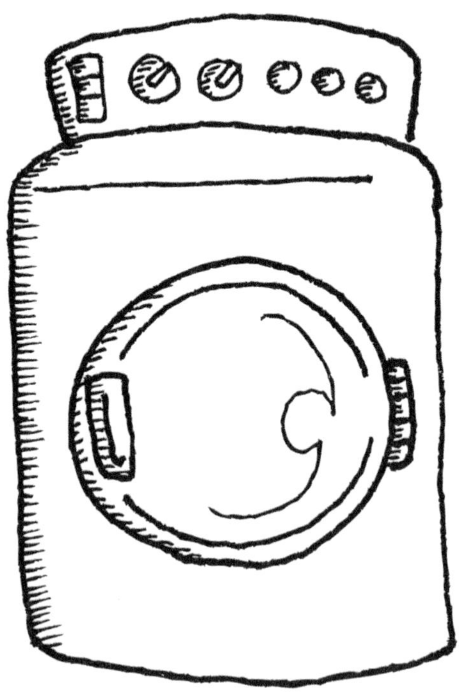

Anyway, I was buying from the company that had the contract to get rid of all the old broken washing machines. I made sure I was down the yard in Coventry when the lorries arrived every week, to cherry pick all the best washing machines. Don't think these were all really old washing machines either, most of them were between 14 months and three years old, just outside the warranty period.

When a washing machine starts playing up, we're so scared off with the engineer call-out charges that many of us just go out and buy a new one. But 90% of the time, there is nothing wrong with the washing machine and it just needs the filter cleaning, which to be fair only takes a couple of minutes. A clogged filter can cause an array of symptoms from clothes not coming out clean to an unbalanced spin to flooding your whole house.

As I'm sat here typing this, I'm grinning from ear to ear reminiscing about my days as a washing machine engineer......those were the days, haha! I have some stories, let me tell you! Maybe not for this book though, but keep your eye out for my next edition, called **Confessions of washing machine engineer.** *Over 18's only, haha!*

So I'm paying around £10 and occasionally spending up to £10 on parts to completely recondition each washing machine. We'd offer three or four different prices. For £89 you got something very basic about three years old, but it did the job and you'd get a six month guarantee. The next one up was £110, we'd always make sure you'd get at least a 1000rpm spin speed on this one. Then £130 would get you something very modern with variable spin speed up to 1200rpm. Occasionally something special would come along with flashing lights that looked like it was a part of the Starship Enterprise, there would always be someone who would part with £150 for it. Still only cost me £10 though. We were very conscious that things could turn in exactly the same way that happened with the televisions, so we were watching the market closely.

Keeping to form, we wanted to move as many washing machines as possible which meant we wanted to supply the trade too, but we needed to fix washing machines quicker than we were, and without employing any staff. You're going to love this next business.

6: How to sell your knowledge

So how do you up productivity and increase revenue without employing more staff? Set up a training school and teach people how to do what we do. Genius, and I cannot take all the glory because it was my dad's idea, to be fair. There is no recognised qualification in being a domestic appliance engineer, well not as far as we knew at the time. A washing machine is nothing more than a drum, a drive motor, a pump and a programme selector with a wiring loom. It fills with water, it heats it, it rotates and then it rinses and spins, it's so simple I could teach primary school children how to build one.

Because I was still quite young and green behind the ears, I don't think the mature students would have taken me seriously on day one when teaching the theory, so I left that to my dad. On days two to four, I trained the students on the practical side of things. To be completely honest, one day theory and one day practical is enough, but when you have 10 or more students who are fully accomplished in reconditioning washing machines, you make the most of it and get them to fix all your stock, haha! But you tell them it's good practice for them.

So how did we find these students who wanted to learn how to become washing machine engineers? We put an advert in Exchange & Mart and also a free magazine which was targeted at our troops; ex-army guys who were leaving the forces, typically they were around mid to late 40s and unemployed, but they had a bit of money to invest in a business venture. For £899 you could train to become a washing machine engineer and we'd show you how to go out there and charge £60+ call out charges to fix broken washing machines, and to recondition your own broken stock for re-sale.

Obviously we did not set anyone up in our local area, as that would have been stupid. We'd have a high enough demand to hold a training course twice a month. The week before a course, I'd make sure we'd have at least 200 faulty washing machines in stock, ready to be reconditioned the following week by our students, that's 20 machines per student. The course would start Monday morning, and by Thursday afternoon, all the washing machines would be fixed. On Friday we'd have a load of cleaners in making the appliances look aesthetically acceptable for sale, which I would then take the next week or two selling. So do the maths: 10 students at £899 each, minus £2000 for stock, but then we'd sell this stock for anything between £50 each to the trade and up to £130 each to the public. Not bad for a lad aged about 19/20, but there's more!

7: A fashion diversion

When I was around 19 years old, I was starting to fulfill my materialistic desires. I always had a wedge of notes in my pocket; I was one of those people who carried a magic wallet, also known as a milkman's wallet, google it if you don't know what I mean. I think I just got a kick out of people's reactions when I pulled a couple of grand out of my pocket as if it was nothing. I'd laugh if I saw someone do that now, I don't know what I was thinking, but I was young. After owning a few dodgy Ford Escorts, I was behind the wheel of my first real sports car when I was 19. A Black Toyota MR2 Mk1, it was about 7 years old and I can't believe I'm going to say this, but it was a complete babe magnet. I felt very successful and must have had male testosterone oozing out of me. As far as I was concerned I was a real catch.

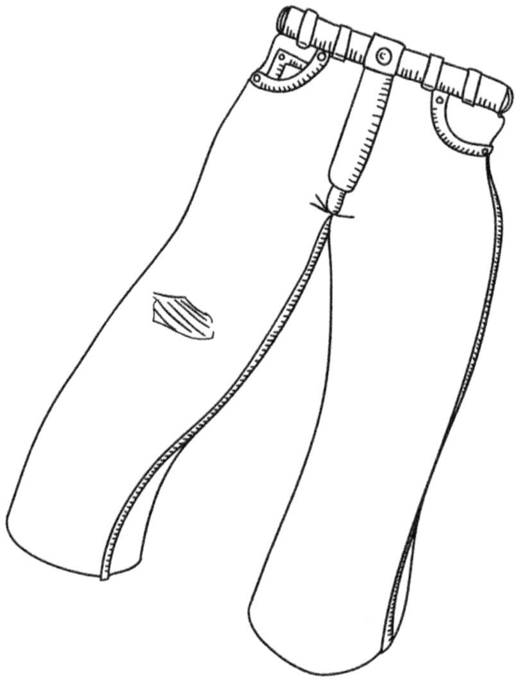

Anyway, back to the business in hand, my girlfriend back then, I'm not going to name her but she knows who she is, but back then she had a passion for clothes, what girl doesn't? And Levi's jeans in particular. A new pair of Levi's 501 jeans would cost about £50, but there was this clothes shop in Oxford selling old pre worn Levis 501's for anything between £80 and £120. I couldn't believe how busy this shop was, they were making a killing. Old pre-worn jeans with rips and tears in them sold for nearly twice as much as a new pair.

So what do you think I did? I bought an Exchange & Mart and went hunting for these jeans. It didn't take me long to find someone selling them; an import agent in Chelsea was shipping them in from the USA for £1 a pair. The only catch was, I had to buy two pallet loads.

Five or six weeks later, two pallets of pressure packed pre worn jeans were dropped on my mum and dad's drive way. Dad was cool with it, he was in on it anyway but mum needed sweetening a little; some flowers did the trick. So here was the plan; to sell them at market stalls, or exhibition halls in hotels with advertising in the local paper a week before hand.

Damn I wish Ebay was around back then, I really would have cleaned up.

Two pallets of jeans was basically 1,000 pairs. Have you ever seen what 1,000 pairs of jeans look like? It didn't look like 500 pairs sitting there on each pallet, until we cut the straps that is: BOOM it was like a steering wheel airbag going off. Hundreds of pairs of jeans filled my parents driveway and garage - good job it was a double garage!

The jeans were so creased there was no way we could sell them like this, so off we went to Argos and bought an iron and ironing board each and we got ironing. I even got my mum involved. Unfortunately, we had to take the rough with the smooth, in other words, out of the 1,000 pairs we could only sell about two thirds of the stock because the other third would be odd sizes which we just couldn't shift. The jeans that were selling, were selling for £40 to £60 so throwing a third of the stock away was not really hurting us. Don't forget we were still running the washing machine business, the jeans were just a bit of fun.

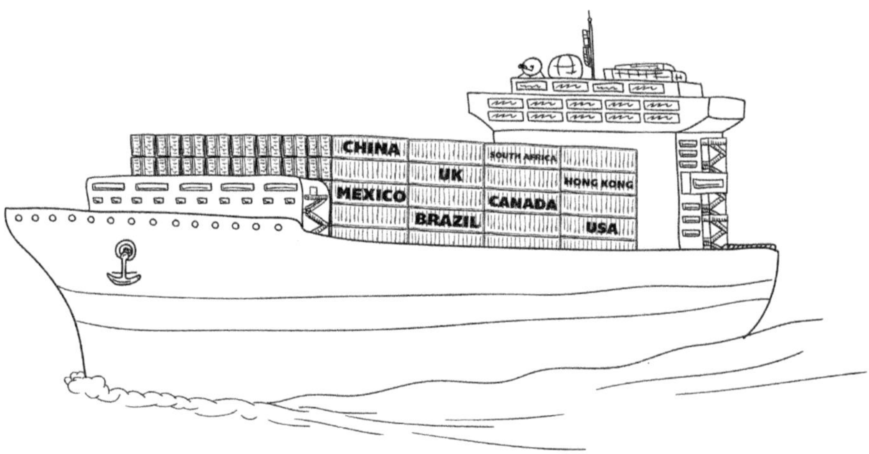

After I had got rid of all the jeans I bought another batch, but this time the import agent in Chelsea asked if she could come up to Banbury to meet us. Her name was Sandra. Over a coffee we discussed many things but there are two things I mainly remember: first, the jeans were from USA prisons - in the USA, apparently Levi's jeans are like a uniform in the prisons for the inmates. And second, she asked what kind of business was I involved in, so when I mentioned washing machines, her eyes lit up. She went on to explain she had contacts in developing countries that had trained as domestic appliance engineers but they needed old broken washing machines to fix and recondition.

I wasn't too sure where this was leading at the time, until she cut to the chase and asked me if I could get hold of hundreds of faulty washing machines on a regular basis. I said sure! I knew I could get my hands on as many as she wanted, so based on my current £10 base cost I quoted her something like £20 a unit, but also said based on the predicted volumes, I'll be able to get back to you later that day with a revised figure hopefully. I called my supplier in Coventry, it was one of those calls where I felt a little silly because I knew he thought I was living in cloud cuckoo land and it would come to nothing, nevertheless he quoted me £5 a unit based on me filling a 40ft container to the hilt. I went back to Sandra with £17 a unit, and she took it.

Within a couple of weeks I was loading containers with washing machines and they were being shipped to destinations in Russia, Nigeria and Bulgaria. There is a bit of red tape in the export game so I never tried bypassing the agent, I knew she was making her cut and it worked well, until it all got a bit annoying. We were loading containers twice a week, so we took on a storage unit/training workshop in Coventry. The timing was perfect as the lease on the unit in Banbury was coming to an end, so I was now commuting everyday from Banbury to Coventry; it was worth it because the rent and rates were so much cheaper.

If any of you know Coventry, and don't forget this is around 1995 to 1996, (I remember this because I had just started seeing a new girlfriend, who I ended up marrying in 1998) well I had taken on premises in Hillfields, Coventry. It was a fairly big unit where we could store hundreds of appliances and still run the training workshops. I think Hillfields has improved since I was there, but when I was there between 1995 and 1997, it was an interesting place. I remember my first morning there and I had heard on the radio someone had been shot dead about 500 yards from where we were based. I had lived a sheltered life in Oxfordshire till then.

I was about to tell you why the exporting got annoying; the clients from the various developing countries wanted to come over and hand pick their appliances the day the container was being loaded, it really messed up our operations. Then, without warning, battered old cars and motorbikes would turn up on the back of a truck and the client would insist they were loaded onto the containers with the washing machines, resulting in the container holding less washing machines.

After a couple of months of pulling my hair out with it, I decided to introduce my export agent to my supplier and give him the headache. Don't worry, I did very nicely out of the introduction.

8:

The cold front

During all the washing machine selling, training and exporting and selling jeans, I also bought and sold fridges and fridge freezers. But I wasn't as passionate about them in the same way as washing machines. Did I just say I was passionate about washing machines haha? Anyway, I applied the same method again really, but there's one thing I'd like to touch on which I feel was an important lesson.

When I had the shop in Banbury, I kept a few 6ft frost-free fridge freezers in stock at all times. Frost-free was quite new back then, and they'd easily set you back £500 in the shops. I was buying these in about 14 months old for £75, and I had them in the shop window for £175, with a six month guarantee. They were like new.

I'd sell at least one a week whereas I was selling 18 to 20 washing machines a week to the public, so I tried an experiment which will prove to you, customers are NOT as price sensitive as you may think, no matter how much they tell you they are. When my mum and dad went on holiday, I put an advert in the paper which said the following: "As new Frost Free Fridge Freezer, was £499, now £299. Please call XXXX". I could not believe how many times that phone rang. I'm chuckling as I'm typing this, as it was a genius idea.

Lucky for me my parents had not long had a brand-new fitted kitchen with integrated appliances, so when the first person turned up to see the advertised frost-free fridge freezer sitting in the middle of the kitchen, plugged in and working and I'd say: "My parents only bought it about 14 months ago, but my mum wanted one of those integrated fridge freezers with her new kitchen so this one is surplus to requirements." It was all very believable. They always tried to negotiate on price, but I'd just say: "Well, someone else is coming round in half an hour (which was true, haha!) and I'd like to see if I can get full price for it."

They'd end up paying me there and then for it and taking it away with them in the back of the car with the seat folded down. Sold as seen, no delivery, no guarantee and I made £125 more profit than I would if I sold it through the shop with free delivery and a six month guarantee. As soon as the fridge freezer was loaded into the car and they had driven off, I was in the garage getting another one out ready for my next buyer. I usually had about four or five lined up in the garage, and I would shift all of them on a Saturday morning.

Was this a scam? I don't think so, I just found a way to sell my stock. Those particular customers obviously had a stigma about buying from a secondhand shop. The product they were actually getting from me was better than a standard second hand appliance, because it had been serviced, but they weren't aware of that.

Lesson learnt here is, don't be the cheapest, package your product or service in a different way, which is unique and desirable to others.

9: Is this a business, or a job?

Ok, time out, I mentioned earlier I met a new girlfriend in 1995 that later I married in 1998. I'm afraid I've fallen into the same stats as most entrepreneurs; later separated in 2009 and divorced in 2010. It's a depressing story, so I won't go there, but I do believe we meet people at different times of our lives for a reason. Things happen for a reason and it's how we deal with it that makes the difference. I regard my ex-wife and I to be extremely lucky to have been given two beautiful daughters, Jasmine and Sophie, who have got the best of the both of us.

Like any guy, when he's in love, everything else takes a back seat; and I remember my concentration was more on my love life than on my business. Although my business paid me very well, there were always highs and lows, which affected cash flow. When you're self-employed, cash flow can determine if you pay yourself on the same date each month. There were many months where this might happen and I suppose because I allowed it to stress me and I couldn't hide this stress, I'd talk about it to my partner.

I'm thinking out aloud here but would I be right in thinking that most people who are employed, who are used to getting paid on the same date each month, would find my situation quite scary?

> *I was encouraged to consider the idea of throwing it all in and getting a proper job, to be employed and working for £18,000 a year, 9 to 5 in a crumby sales job. I can't believe I actually considered it.*

It didn't help when I was occasionally hearing on the grapevine that people thought I was a bit of a Del Boy, and this was coming from my girlfriend's side of the family.

But really it just made me more determined to prove them all wrong. Christmases were hilarious, when the cousin's boyfriends were displayed like commodities. It was all done in good taste but there was an undertone of which daughter has the best boyfriend. No pressure?! Anyway you'll be glad to know I did not concede under the pressure and I stuck to my guns and stayed self employed.

In 1998, aged 23, we got married. During 1997 my dad and I started to work more independently. He went off and started a computer business. He was mad about computers and loved building them from scratch. He got so good at it, he applied a similar method we had applied to the other businesses. He started of by building them and selling them, and then he ran one day training courses which then became full week training courses depending on how much you wanted to learn, from simple building and configuring a tower PC through to gaining a recognised qualification in something to do with computers.

I wasn't really that interested, but I do remember him banging on about this new thing which was either already around or was about to be launched called the "World Wide Web". As far as I was concerned it was just another geeky thing for geeky nerds to be concerned about, who played on computers all night and didn't have a life. I find it a little scary when I think back to this memory, that little did I know I'd end up running a multi-million pound business on this thing called the World Wide Web.

Another memory I have from 1999 is when I was quite proud of the fact that I was one of those people that decided people who spent so much time on their computers, were sad individuals and didn't have a life. It wasn't until mid 1999 when I decorated the spare bedroom in Hillside Close, Banbury so I had an office where I could do my bookkeeping for my washing machine business. Someone had told me about Microsoft Office and how it would help me create invoices and other funky stuff to help me with my business, so I had succumbed to owning my first PC (which my dad built for me). That was it, I was hooked. I was one of those men who sat up stairs all night spending time on my computer.

10: Decide on your passions

Ok I've told you I am the founder of a multi million pound company, this is true, but don't confuse this with self-made millionaire, this is something I do not consider myself, well not yet. Although my company turns over a few million pounds a year, I am sure as hell not paying myself anywhere near that kind of salary. Don't misunderstand me, I pay myself very well so I don't go with out; I live in a nice home and have regular exotic holidays with a few European city breaks thrown in there too. I like to change my car every 12 to 18 months and it's always something luxurious and sporty.

Then there's my real passion, my real selfish love affair with my motorbike. May God keep me safe! If I had my way I'd fill my garage with all sorts of bikes, from GP sports bikes right down to vintage Royal Enfields and Triumph Bonnevilles. I just love motorbikes. There's something about hitting the road for a few hours. When you have your helmet on, it's like you're in your own little bubble and it's a great place for me to unwind and de-stress.

Back to my main point. The way my current company is growing I am sure it will eventually one day enable me to draw sufficient funds from it so I have in excess of a million pounds in my personal bank account, but that's not the plan. If I take out that kind of money from the business, well then I'm affecting the growth of the company. The challenge is to grow the company and then sell it when I'm out of steam or bored and want to move onto another project.

Actually it's not that simple. I don't know about you but I am one of those entrepreneurs that get bored easily. One of the things I have learnt is that you should not necessarily stick at something and work through the boredom. My best work is usually achieved when I am really passionate about something, the feeling you get when sleep and food become an inconvenience as it distracts you from what you are working so passionately on.

If you know what I am talking about then you've just proved to yourself you have the drive to succeed. You just have to make sure it's something you're really passionate about. So to cut to the chase, I probably have grown tired of my current company, I've done my bit, I got it started, I worked those long hours from 6.30am right through to 2am, occasionally surviving on only four hours sleep. But I didn't see this as hard work, I was doing something I strongly believed in and I was seeing the results week on week, month on month.

The reason I have not sold the business yet is because this is the first business where I have embraced the power of delegation. Wow, after 16 years of being in business and having eight businesses along the way, it's taken me this long to delegate roles and processes within the company. I've managed to grow it to a size where I am no longer needed. In other words, it runs without me, even better, it's growing without me too. So I am in no real hurry to sell at the moment. So I just draw a modest salary, which covers my living expenses, but it's nice knowing I can take more from the business if I really needed to but the challenge is to resist and don't be too greedy.

Ha, I can hear some of you saying: "Steve says don't be too greedy, yet he's got all those nice things." That's right, it's about getting the balance right. I hold my hands up to the fact

I am materialistic, and I shamefully measure some of my success by having nice things. For me it's a bit of a driver and I'll talk about goals and rewards later in the book, but for now you must accept there is no shame in treating yourself to the luxuries in life, especially if you've worked hard for them. People do judge me and look down on me - I've even had a random person spit on my car out of jealousy, what's the world coming to? These people don't stop and think: "I wonder if that successful person does any good with his money and his time?"

This is where the magic really starts happening; the more successful I become, the more I can do for charities. My company carries out thousands of transactions each day, so we support worthwhile causes by offering a "Round up your Pound" service at its checkout. We regularly say "Keep the change", so why not do something useful with it online? We'll tell you what your order total is - let's say it's £8.60, then give you the option to round up to £9.00. If you say yes, we'll give the spare 40p to charity. It won't be a lot to you, but it will be a lot for the charity when all the other customers add their spare change too.

We have helped so many worthwhile causes with this. I would not be able to do something on this scale if my company was not successful. We also plant hundreds of new trees every year to help with the environment. But one of the main things that really gives me that little buzz, is that I am an employer keeping people in jobs. This was not something I set out to do, but it's something which has had to happen organically, as the business has grown.

Speaking of staff, although it's nice to know that my business has created many jobs, something which took me a little while to figure out is that I am no good interviewing or managing staff, so I've delegated that role to someone else. Only two or three of my staff are original employees from when I first started the company, everyone else was interviewed and is managed by someone else in the company. I'll talk about this a bit more later in the book, as this was a huge learning curve for me.

11: How this book's title came about

There's an analogy I like to use when I am speaking to audiences; it's clear I claim not to have the same success as Alan Sugar or Richard Branson. These guys are exceptional. We look up to these people in awe, and wonder what it must be like to achieve such grandeur and wealth. It's not impossible, but it is a long shot.

Follow me with this one. We're all fish in the sea. The likes of Sugar and Branson are far out in the deep ocean. We can barely see them because they are so far ahead of us. All the start up and small businesses are swimming in the breakers. Crashing waves are constantly throwing the small fish back onto the shore, or even worse, getting smashed against the rocks causing cuts and bruises. The challenge for these small fish is to swim as hard as possible through all the waves to eventually reach the calm deeper waters.

There are fewer fish in the calm deeper waters, but these fish know only too well what it's like to be swimming in the crashing waves, because it was either not that long ago; or although they're in the calm waters now, they haven't continued their journey further to go and chase the really big fish that are far out in the distance on the horizon, and probably on their yacht! So the rough choppy waters are right behind them, and it's easy to slide back in there if they're not careful.

> *I regard myself as one of the fish that has made it through the breakers, but I've got 15 plus years of experience of what it's like being smashed against the rocks with the scars to prove it. I now have a clearer site of the yachts on the horizon, something new to aim for.*

Although it's inspiring hearing about the really big fish, I'd like to think I can offer motivation to new businesses and inspiration to established companies that can relate to the similar challenges I have faced. I consider that I am in touching distance for many smaller, lifestyle businesses.

Where I am, is the next realistic achievable step, and not a pipe dream. I'm now in the luxurious position where I no longer need to work. I've structured my business that way so I can now do what I enjoy instead of doing things I have to do.

I felt the book title set the right tone, and tested it on a few friends – with some very interesting results! The most extraordinary was from my daughters Jasmine and Sophie, who shouted out "Cardboard box" the second they heard it.

Sounds random? Not if you're a child of a certain age – and perhaps a doting parent who watches TV with them, too. It appears that Bob the Builder and his friends have a song, complete with hand jive moves, with the fairly unfathomable lyrics: "Big fish, little fish, cardboard box". Check it out on YouTube, if you like.

So if you felt inclined to shout "Cardboard box" the moment you saw this book, you're forgiven. We're all big kids inside – and we can usually trust the kids to bring our lofty ideas back down to earth!

Me and my girls.

12: When you're out of your depth, cut your losses

If you remember, I got to about age 21 when I had met my wife to be. With all of the ups and downs of running your own businesses, I listened to her concerns and reeled in my entrepreneurial flair and just fixed washing machines for a living.

> *I wasn't thinking it at the time but looking back I was surrounding myself with people who accepted one or two employed jobs in life and they lived to their means. If they wanted something badly they would either save for it or they would accept they would never be able to have it, and go without.*

All a bit boring really, and not really enjoying this gift of life and seeing what you can achieve in the short time we're here. We live on an amazing planet and I sure don't want to be on my death bed one day knowing I haven't explored most of it. Living in the same old town for the rest of my life would drive me nuts. Each to their own, though.

So between 21 and 23 years it was all about wedding plans and buying our first house, there was nothing exciting going on with the business. I was just repairing broken washing machines for a living. At 23 years old, I was happy and content living in our first house, but niggling me at the back of my head were some of my dreams in life; I really wanted an AC Cobra, but this just didn't fit in with what our joint plans were, so I came to the conclusion I wasn't going to be getting one anytime soon. I still don't have one now, but to be honest, wants and needs change so frequently in life, you have to keep updating your business and reward plans as and when you feel appropriate, just to keep you driven if anything.

I no longer have a desire for an AC Cobra, so even if I could have afforded it when I was 23, I'd have probably got bored of it before I was 24, but I'd have had new goals and rewards lined up throughout my twenties after I had bought that car. I have so much more to expand on here when it comes to business plans, goals and rewards, but I'll come on to that later in the book. You really need to read on and learn about my business plan strategies, they're fun, but more importantly they work. If I ever decide to mentor anybody, the main focus will be on the rewards in life they desire. I say if ever, I already mentor a few people now for free, but it's just to see if they value my help and if my methods work for others, plus I get such a kick out of it.

So I'm accepting my new life, married, three bedroom house, holidays to Europe as and when we can afford it. Don't misunderstand me, I was happy, I just knew I had certain things I wanted to achieve in life which my other half didn't share with me. I tried my hardest to suppress those life time achievements that I wanted to reach and I was coming round to the realisation that I'd never achieve them and I had to be realistic and be happy with what I've got.

After all, this is what was being told to me all the time by close family. I must also stress this.

> *Close family weren't being negative because they didn't like me. If anything it's because they care; and above all of that, it's because they're scared of anything that is different.*

This is why we see so many people follow a similar path to their parents, not always an identical path, but not too dissimilar. It's very rare when you see someone completely smash the mould, and I want to tell you about a very special person in my life who is a huge inspiration to me. Someone who grew up in modest surroundings, had no real successful role models in her family to follow and somehow she has climbed the corporate ladder and earns an incredible salary which makes me look tiny. I'll tell you more about her later too, as it's an incredible journey she has been on.

After a few of years of marriage, I'm 26, I've gone from a lean 14 stone adonis to a 17 stone something whale. Ahh...contentment everybody says. Why has everybody got an excuse for when things are looking bad? Being told it was contentment was like being given permission to get fatter, so I did. Think about it, my day job was being a washing machine engineer. I was on the road all day stopping at burger vans and petrol stations, picking up those multi deal offers on chocolate bars. Eating four king size chocolate bars in one sitting was not difficult for me. I appreciate I was married and should not be concerned if other women were checking me out or not, the point is, they weren't and I was not liking what I was seeing in the mirror. Something had to change and I'm not just talking about my weight and fitness.

On top of all this, we wanted to start a family. This was a huge pressure on me. In one hand I wanted to give my wife what she wanted, and in the other hand I had all my dreams spiraling down the plug hole, but to be fair I wasn't doing anything about it, so I was the only one to blame, but I sure was stuck in a rut. A path which life was dictating to me, instead of a life which I was dictating which path I took.

> *Are you on a path that life is dictating to you or are you on a path that you have full control of, therefore your life is going in the direction you choose? Understanding this on a deep level will motivate you.*

Whilst we were expecting our first child, I needed to get my entrepreneurial head back in gear. I dabbled with cars and got my fingers seriously burnt. I know nothing about cars, not on a technical or mechanical level anyway, I just like driving them. Can you imagine what I was up against at home when I had to tell her I'd bought a car for £8,000, spent £2,000 on repairs but then couldn't sell it for anything more than £8,000? I can't remember if that was the exact maths, but I made a significant loss.

The business idea wasn't anything new, it was buying catergory D write off cars with minor damage, getting them fully restored and selling them still as Cat D restored cars. My first car was an Escort RS Turbo convertible, with minor wing damage but later I discovered the wiring loom all needed replacing and there was damage under the car, so what I thought was going to cost a few hundred quid, ended up being a couple of thousand pounds.

Long term plan was to move on to higher end vehicles like TVRs and Porsches but I wasn't getting the support at home to do it again, plus the money just wasn't there to fund it. I was not very popular at all really. Remember my fish analogy, this was me charging into the waters with too much haste, and the very first wave that came along caught me and threw me very hard against the rocks, hard enough to make me stop with that idea, but not hard enough to stop me with something else.

13:

How to really get into debt

As a washing machine repairman, I was meeting all sorts of people, from lonely housewives, to hotel and guest house managers through to landlords who needed washing machines for their lettings. Two people in particular inspired me: one guy, Phil Jones had been a landlord all his life, having started when he was very young and bought his first house in Coventry. Thirty or so years on, he owns the entire street, and this is when I met him. He needed me to put a washing machine into each letting; each house had about four or five lettings, and there were about 40 houses in the street. Nice deal eh! But me being me, I asked him how he started his business and tried to find out how I could replicate what he'd done.

Also around the same time I met a guy called Martin, a similar age to me driving a brand-new BMW M3 convertible which he changed every year. Martin was a huge inspiration to me. His main business was being an independent financial advisor (IFA), but his passion was property. He was buying new flats and apartments about three times a year all across the Stratford-Upon-Avon area, and he also needed washing machines for his lettings. I got to know Martin quite well and basically asked him to help me get started with a property portfolio.

When I get an idea in my head I don't like to hang about, I found my first buy-to-let property in Banbury, right by the college. It was a five bedroom, four storey house. My intention was to let it out to five students but for all of them to jointly sign one contract. If anyone of you know a bit about HMO's (houses in multiple occupancy) you'll know the hoops that need to be jumped through, however, the money is good, as long as they're all paying their rent. I was lucky that house prices were rising, I managed to release over £30,000 on my current property so I had the deposit for the buy-to-let, the mortgage on the buy-to-let was for about £130,000 and the monthly payments were less than £600 per month. Rent was £250 per month per person, so I was turning over £1,250 per month in total leaving me with a profit of about £650. It wasn't long until I bought the next house, just around the corner.

Can you imagine how I was feeling? I had stood my ground and ignored all negativity about starting a property portfolio. I was confronted with what if's all the time from various people around me. What if this goes wrong, what if that happens, what if your tenants can't pay you, what if what if what if. I use to reply with: "What if it all goes really well and I grow a great big property portfolio and I end up getting disgustingly rich, what then?" The response would be something like: "Well Stephen, that's all well and good, but that's not how life pans out, you have to be realistic otherwise you'll end up losing everything and where would you be then?" Such comments deliver a great lesson:

> *Although we should respect our elders, people with more life experience than ourselves, don't take advice from them if they're not from where you are aspiring to be.*

If you want to start your own company and have dreams of growing it into a big business, then ask for advice from people who have already been there and done it. You'll find your family and loved ones will give you their advice without you even asking for it. They do this because they care and they don't want to see you get hurt or hurt the people around you. These people who reflect negativity have more experience in meeting the people who have failed in setting up their business, this is because all of the successful business owners are mixing in different circles. It's harsh, but it's true. By submerging yourself in and among the successful people, it'll have an affect on you and you'll end up joining them.

I'm such a typical entrepreneur, I can't keep on track, I keep going off on tangents. I apologise, but I hope you're enjoying it and getting nuggets of information you can use to make a positive change in your life and business.

So at this stage I'm still a washing machine repairman but now I have a property portfolio. With the house I live in, and the buy-to-lets I've bought, I've got about half a million mortgaged. This didn't scare me one bit but I really enjoyed telling my mum, she was freaking out. But here's the icing on the cake, my dad did something that blew me away. I talked a bit about my dad earlier in the book, he's a very proud man, but for some reason he struggled with telling me he was proud of me or telling me he loves me. I think it's an old school thing so I make allowances for him, haha! Anyway, he presented me with his very own Rolex watch which he'd treated himself to a few years before hand but now he was handing it over to me to show me how proud he was of me. He told me he was proud of me. Wow, no money or achievement can beat that feeling. As I write this, my eyes are welling up. I'm not ashamed to display my emotions; I can be a right cry baby when I'm happy.

14: Time to take another risk

Also around about now, a friend mentioned the name Anthony Robbins to me. He had bought two CD sets, "Get The Edge" and "Unleash the Power Within". He was going nuts about these CDs, telling me I needed to get them to help me in my businesses. They were expensive, and I thought there couldn't be anything so important on those CDs that it would help me become a millionaire, so didn't plan to waste my hard earned money.

Because he was a friend I thought I'd ask him if he'd consider burning me some copies. Some friend, he burned them for me but negotiated a deal so I was paying half what he had to pay, which is fair, but I wouldn't have done that to a friend.

Anyway, enough said about that because if he's reading this, he knows who he is. So I briefly listened to the CDs and it sounded like a load of cobblers, all about self belief, happy clappy and all that fluffy stuff.

However, I subjected myself to these CDs everyday in my van. Yes, that's right folks, I had a CD player in my Citroen Berlingo Van, it was a 2001 X reg, Del Boy and Rodney would have been wel jel (well jealous). I remember when Robbins said, stop the tape and start writing things down, I didn't bother, it's because I wasn't taking it seriously - but I did enjoy listening to what he had to say, and it was rubbing off on me. Those of you who noticed I said it was CDs but Robbins said stop the tape, that is because these seminars and workshops must have been recorded right back in the day before CDs were even invented.

Taking on board some of the things Robbins talked about, I started looking for another business idea. You're going to love this one, this always goes down very well when I'm speaking at an event. Without any knowledge of horse racing (I'd never even stepped inside a bookies), I thought I'd be qualified enough to become a professional horse racing tipster. Seriously, I had no idea what all these phrases meant, like the going was good to firm, I remember asking someone what was the "Going"?. I also had to learn how to figure out all the odds like evens, 5/4, 3/1 so I knew what horse had what value and what return you'd get based on a £100 stake.

Once I'd equipped myself with this knowledge, I set up my first ever website called www.ggtips.net. I then placed an advert in the Daily Mirror, a very small box advert advertising "Professional Tipster, call now for free inside information". That first day I received about five calls to my mobile phone. Sure enough the tip was completely free, all I was doing was watching the best tipsters in the paper that were picking winners with odds better than 3/1.

Now you're probably thinking where's the money in this? Well although the tip was free, I'd ask the caller to place £5 on the horse on my behalf. If the horse wins, you need to special delivery the winnings in cash to me by tomorrow morning, that way you'll qualify for the next tip.

Sure enough that first tip was a winner. I can categorically remember I never had a caller not send me the winnings. I used to have anything from £90 to £900 cash landing on my doorstep, three times a week. I'd always update the website after a race too, so all my callers could see I wasn't fabricating good results. Because you can't pick a winner every day, I came up with betting systems which I advised my callers to use, so even though they were betting on five horses a week, they'd still be up on their profits if only two horses won. I of course wasn't gambling - it's a mug's game - I was just offering a service to gamblers.

Unfortunately I couldn't sustain this business. On a couple of occasions I was giving out eight or nine losers in a row; it wasn't intentional but when this happened I was getting threatening phone calls. All of my callers knew my home address and I had an 18 month old daughter with another one on the way, so I think I made the right decision ending it, but I had a good six month run at it and it was lots of fun too. I'd say this is the scammiest business I set up, and one which I'm sure Del Boy would be proud of too.

15:

How some people really miss a trick

I've now got a daughter at this stage and also we were expecting another. Jasmine would have been about 18 months old and Sophie was due in the September, which means it's around the spring of 2003. It was a Sunday morning and we've decided to gather lots of clutter together and take it down to the local car boot sale. Now I really cannot stand car boot sales, walking around a field looking at other people's old tat in the back of their cars just isn't my thing, but I've always got my eye out, open for the next big thing. Actually that's something to take note on - I'm not a big believer in finding a product or service that hasn't been invented yet:

> *If you are in that position where you have an idea that's never been tested or invented, then you're taking on a huge job to get it off the ground, because no one knows about it.*

The cost of getting the nation to learn about your new thing will not be cheap, but that said, don't let that stop you, if you truly believe it will work and you've done your market research and you've got the determination and passion to make it work, then you will make it happen. I like to stumble upon ideas that are already out there and working for others, and then mimic what they're doing - or do it better, if you believe you can.

There was a man at the car boot sale selling tiny motorised motorbikes, which were really cool. They were basically mini versions of the motorbikes you see on the road today, or on the race track and their official name is mini moto's. I could see from where my stall was he was selling them one after the other, so I walked over to investigate.

He was selling them for about £250, they actually had mini petrol engines, they were noisy little things and bloody dangerous too, but kids and adults loved them and they were selling well. People who know me in business know I'm cheeky, and my cheekiness has won me deals and got me into places that just wouldn't have happened if I'd kept my mouth shut. In this instance I asked him outright how much was he buying them for. I was expecting him to say "On Yer Bike" - excuse the pun! But like a fool he told me.

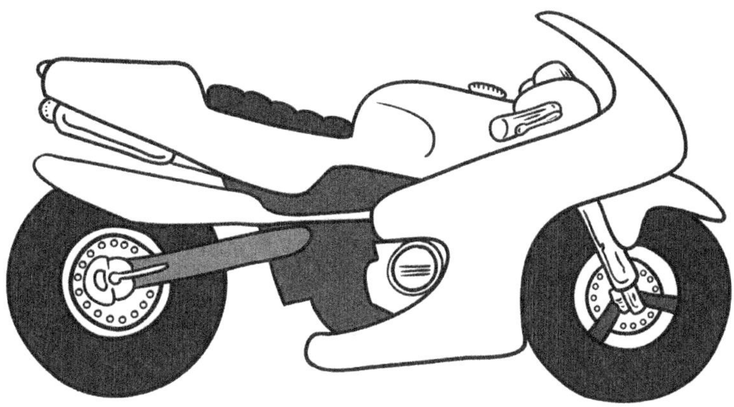

He was making a very good margin of 150% but I appreciate he had to spend a lot of time preparing the bikes for sale, as they weren't exactly ready to ride out of the box. I then followed up with another question, asking him where did he buy them from? Well I thought if he told me how much he's paying, he might end up telling me where from. I was pushing my luck, but he did say he had to buy ten bikes at a time to get them for the low price he was paying.

So I went away and started my research, finding out where these little bikes are made. They're basically replica bikes made in China. The original bikes made by Blata in Czech Republic are very expensive and high quality bikes, but the Chinese thought they would make a cheaper alternative.

I looked at the possibility of buying them direct from China but limited cash reserves put a stop to that. I'd have had to buy a 40 foot container full of them, then deal with the import duties and storage facilities, so I had to rule that one out, but this would have been the cheapest option for me. I found two suppliers, one up in Preston and one down in Exeter, they were both buying direct from China, from different sources. After a phone call to both of them I went to go and see them to discuss prices and volume. At this stage I had already painted this picture in my head of this website called Xtremewheels, displaying an array of bikes and selling them to the public and the trade, as long as I can get the deal with the wholesalers.

Bearing in mind I hadn't got any orders yet, it took some convincing them that I was going to be buying regular high volumes from them. Initially I wasn't interested in handling the bikes, I wanted to advertise them on my website and then as and when I sold one, I would arrange to have it shipped directly from the wholesaler to my customer.

Anyway, I negotiated well based on volume across the month and not based on per order, like the guy at the car boot. Within a week of meeting that guy at the car boot, I had done all of my research and had my meetings. I took pictures of the bikes at the wholesalers, to create a temporary brochure to show retailers whilst I was setting up my new Xtremewheels website. The guy at the car boot was buying from me already and I was saving him £5 per bike and getting them shipped directly to his door. I could have sold them one at a time but seeing as he told me he had to buy 10 at a time, I said he had to buy five at a time, so we were both happy.

I remember working through the night getting the website ready. I am self-taught in web design, I had to do it myself as web design wasn't cheap in 2003. I used Dreamweaver and SmartFTP to create and update pages. I believe it's a lot easier to create websites these days though. I kept it simple, making the bikes as easy as possible to view and buy.

To beat the competition out there on the internet, I did something very different which eventually got copied. I got in touch with a graphics company who'd normally sell a graphics set for your bike for £30. I managed to get them for £2.50 a set, because I was ordering so many. I had to get some bikes in stock at my house, so I could apply the graphics and take good quality photographs for the website. So when you came to my site you could view and buy a mini replica of Valentino Rossi's Moto GP bike, or you could buy a Honda Fireblade or a Yamaha R1, plus many more. By doing this I could charge £50 more than my competitors and still get the business. It's also worth knowing that I didn't need to apply the graphics to each bike I sold, that would have been impossible as the bikes were being dropped shipped. When an order came in, the customer would receive the bike from one location and the graphics would be sent from another location. I made this clear in my terms, plus it's more enjoyable if you apply the decals yourself.

Now for the numbers. I was eventually buying these bikes for £60 plus vat, plus £25 to have them drop shipped. So my total cost was £85. In my first year I was selling them for between £299 to £349. In my second year, I had to review my prices due to strong competition so they came down to £199 to £249. I was selling anything from 20-60 of these bikes a week, depending on the time of year. You can imagine Christmas was busy.

16: You're nothing without your health

This was my first real business that was starting to take off, but I was so busy juggling Xtremewheels, Spinspeed and by now I was experiencing problems with some of my tenants in the buy-to-let properties, dealing with non-payers, vandalism and complaints from their neighbours. And to top it off, I had a pregnant wife. I was very stressed and I can recall a few times where I felt like exploding because I couldn't be everywhere at the same time and keep everybody happy. (I don't think I mentioned, when I was married my washing machine business was called SpinSpeed.)

A big wake up call for me was when I was around 28 years old. Although I had got my entrepreneurial hat back on, I hadn't taken control of my weight and fitness, I was a big lad and not far of 18 stone. I was in my Citroen Berlingo doing call out repairs in the Solihull area. I remember thinking it was late, I had already worked the morning at home getting all the bike sales dispatched and dealing with customer enquiries. I had a same day dispatch service if you ordered your bike by 1pm so I couldn't leave the house until 1.30pm at the earliest.

To get a lot of work as a washing machine engineer, I advertised across a 50 mile radius from Banbury, which caused logistical nightmares for me now I was running more than one business. Anyway, it was late and I needed to get back into Banbury to see a tenant, plus I wanted to get back home by a decent time to see my daughter before she went to bed. I hadn't eaten that day, I forgot or I just didn't have the time to stop so I pulled into the MacDonalds on the A34, right by junction 4 on the M42, to grab a quarter pounder meal deal.

I drove through the drive through, grabbed my food and started to head for the car park exit and then I had to suddenly slam on my brakes. A long sharp pain went up my arm and across my chest leaving me frozen for about six seconds for the pain to pass. I felt my heart popping out of my chest, I could hear it loud and clear in my ears and although I was shivering with cold, my top was soaking wet with sweat.

To this day I have never had confirmation of what it was, I spoke to a doctor off the record a few weeks later who said I'd just had a wake up call and I should start taking care of myself. Guess what, I didn't eat the quarter pounder meal, I just sat there for the next hour resting and thanking God I was still alive. There is a history of heart attacks in my family, so I don't really want to push it.

I didn't really slow down, I just watched what I was eating, I went on a Slimming World plan, red and green day diet, which worked well; I lost loads of weight - but I put it all back on again a year later. I really tried to plan out my days better, so I was better organised, until there was another day which was another wake up call which I'll mention shortly.

Remember I said I used to have premises in Coventry when I was about nineteen, shipping appliances internationally through an export agent? Well although I wasn't based out of Coventry when I was 28, I was still visiting the city two to three times a week to pick up washing machines and spares. There was a chap called Barry Masterson who worked at the yard where I use to pick up my washing machines. The best way to describe Barry, if you saw him in the street and you didn't know him, you'd probably be worried he was about to either mug you or kill you. The last thing you'd want to do is look him in the eye.

However, over the years of visiting the yard I got to know Barry and guess what, he's as soft as they come really, but I wouldn't push him. He'd do anything to help me out if I asked him and it turned out he knew loads about cars, bikes, anything with an engine really. He convinced me if I opened a shop in Coventry selling mini moto's I'd clean up, so that's what I did. I took on a shop in Holbrooks, Coventry, next to a launderette.

On one side of the shop I had washing machines and on the other side of the shop I had mini motos. A right real Trotters Enterprise operation, haha. I was still drop shipping, but now I was tying up my time even more by being stuck in a shop in Coventry. Not a wise move looking back, but now I was offering a repair service to your mini moto, which Barry was carrying out. I met some really interesting people in the few short months I was running out of this shop. Firstly the shop got broken into at least three times a week because of the stock in there. I ended up buying a huge Renault Master van, big enough where I could get all my stock into it at the end of the day. You'd see the youths at the corner of the road watching to see if I was emptying the shop at night or not.

A salesman for a popular motorised trail bike company came to see me one day, offering me these very cool 90cc Xsport bikes, they were quick but the same sort of size as a BMX. To cut a long story short I started buying these bikes from him to put in my shop, but they were selling well online too and I was making an easy £100 mark up on them as well.

One day this guy, not much older than myself walks in my shop. He's wearing very nice clothes and he has two body guards with him, I didn't realise they were body guards until after he had left the shop, but he bought two of these new Xsport bikes.

I've been known to be a bit naïve and not get the plot straight away and it wasn't until Barry spelt it out to me as they were jumping in their car. He started by laughing his head off, saying I had just aided a criminal. Barry knew who he was, hence why he disappeared out the back listening through the crack in the door. The penny dropped when I remembered the guy was very specific the bikes had to have an electric start for a quick get away and not a kick start. Well, what was I supposed to do, refuse to sell to a guy who was probably carrying a knife or gun or is the type to arrange a job on me if I didn't comply? I never saw him again, but I'm under no illusion that those bikes were quite possibly used for something illegal.

17: Some advice to ignore, some to heed

Another day in the shop and this very nice Mercedes SL500 AMG with a very expensive private plate rolls up. A chap steps out of the car and comes in to buy two bikes for his sons. Now who knows what these bikes were really for? I don't ask questions.

He asked about the washing machines and asked me if I knew a certain person in Coventry who supplies washing machines, of whom I did know. We were basically networking, but for some reason I had to get my wallet out of my pocket; he asked me how many credit cards I had, and then asked me how much available credit did I have? It all sounded very suspicious. He left saying he'd be in touch with a business proposal later that day.

Before the day was over, my friend who supplied me with my washing machines called me, saying: "Steve, I hear you have met John." He went on to explain John and him went back a long time and knew one another at school, he was a good friend but was a very corrupt businessman and had been inside many times. My friend advised me that John wanted to know if I was interested in the following business deal: to give him my wallet, then report it stolen and stop all my cards 24 hours later. Because my available credit limit was around 100k across all my cards, he was offering me 25k in cash. In the twenty four hours he would buy as much valuable merchandise that he could easily sell on for less than what the shops charge.

This is completely illegal, and I remember my stomach churning as he was telling me. My friend strongly advised me not to get involved even though it was his friend that was running this illegal business. I'll be honest, I was tempted, 25k would have really come in handy and the insurance would have paid out on the cards, apparently.

I'm glad I never did it, but I'm telling you this to give you an idea of the people who I was meeting when working out of Coventry. I suppose this is nothing compared to the time when I had a guy once ask me if I wanted anyone killed for £50. I remember asking him, what about if I just want someone lamed, he replied that'll be £500. So I said: "So, it's cheaper to kill than to lame?" He said: "Of course, when we kill, the victim cannot witness who does it. If we lame them, there's a risk we may get caught." I suppose this stuff does go on, but whether or not he was the real deal or not, I'm not sure.

So I was on my way home one night from Coventry, but I had to stop in at Warwick on the way to change a water pump on a Zanussi washing machine, I was also in a rush again to get back to Banbury to meet a new tenant. The washing machine was on the top floor of a four storey block of flats with no lift. The stairs were wide and made out of smooth polished concrete. When I left the flat I was in such a hurry I remember launching myself from the top steps and jumping the entire flight on each floor, grabbing the hand rail at each corner to take the next flight as quickly as possible. I didn't have my tool case on me as I had already taken this down to the van to take up my receipt book.

On the last flight of stairs the first floor ledge must have been a little lower than the others, as I jumped I was focusing on the floor at the bottom so my head was down, but my head hit the ledge with all my weight behind it, my feet came flying up and I landed on my back at the bottom of the stairs.

It must have knocked me out for a few seconds because the first thing I remember was seeing the guy from the fourth floor flat. He told me to go straight to the hospital to get my head stitched up. The cut was probably only about an inch long but I don't think I have ever seen so much blood come out of me. I didn't go to the hospital in Warwick, I didn't want to park my van with over £15,000 worth of bikes in the back of it in a hospital car park, so I stupidly proceeded to drive thirty miles back to Banbury. By the time I got back home I was red from head to toe, even my shoes and socks were soaked in blood. On that drive to the hospital I made the decision to slow down and not take on as much work. I needed something new, but something that would make more money and I could work less. Little did I know the new venture was just around the corner.

So the mini moto business was still doing really well, albeit the margins were being squeezed. I got rid of the shop and just worked from home, not easy when there's two children under three in the house.

Here's another lesson learnt, Xtremewheels was VAT registered, it was doing well enough whereby I had to be paying and charging VAT. Now I'm not sure how Google do this these days, my business analyst and accountant deals with all that now, but some of you who are in business might relate to what I'm going to share. Now I was very busy, I hate doing the accounts so I was outsourcing that job to an accountant, but because of costs, I still had to do my own bookkeeping. So although I wasn't doing my own VAT return, I had a good idea how much it was going to be each quarter as I was doing my own bookkeeping.

I was the guy who'd collect all my receipts in one draw and then do it all on the last night, it took me hours. It's great writing this as it's reminding me of how much hard work I used to put in back in the early days, whereas now it's all very much more laid back and I delegate almost everything.

Anyway, I use to log in into my Google Adwords account every quarter just to download all my weekly invoices. Adwords was my biggest outgoing in the company so these invoices really needed to be submitted as it affected my VAT bill significantly. Google didn't use to show the VAT amount on their invoices back in 2003 through to 2008, well they didn't for me anyway. But at the bottom of their invoices it stated clearly that the invoice was subjected to self assessment VAT, depending on what country you live in. So the total gross amount at the bottom was the amount I had actually paid, the VAT field was left empty and the net amount above that reflected the same as the gross total.

To anyone looking at this it looks like a VAT exempt invoice and the company isn't charging VAT, but it's Google and they have a VAT number at the top of the invoice and the self assessment declaration at the bottom. So I proceeded to alter the invoices so the net amount was less than the gross amount and the VAT at 17.5% added up to the gross amount which is on my bank statements. Done, easy! I didn't think I'd need to have had a conversation about this with my accountant, as it was pretty self explanatory and they could see where I had crossed out the 0.00 on the VAT field and applied the correct VAT amount.

Now who am I to question my accountant? It used to annoy me that I would generate a VAT figure which was always £1000 less, growing later to around £2,500 less than my accountants worked it out to be, but I just put it down to the fact they knew what they were doing better than me. I just had to work harder to make sure I paid all those VAT bills. Over two years of doing this, in 2006 I sat down with my accountant and said: "This is getting silly, can you tell me why my numbers are so different to yours?" The accountant casually turned his head and said: "It's because you keep changing the Google invoices. It's illegal, you're not allowed to do that."

I still don't know how I didn't throw that guy out of his window. I was fuming, I pointed it out to him where it says about the self assessment VAT and he acknowledged it, but he said: "There's no such thing as self assessment VAT" - so he had ignored it. I sarcastically responded: "Oh so Google don't know what the hell they're doing then and you know better?"

I'm sure you can imagine I fired them and I got a nice VAT rebate. What I think they never understood was, is that for a small business which I was, taking that kind of hit every quarter was crucifying me. It could have killed my business quite easily. I now have a very good chartered accountant based in Oxfordshire, who understands me and my businesses. They do all my bookkeeping and give great advice. A great accountant is very important when you're a growing business, they need to be a bit of a business partner, someone you can use as a sounding board.

18: The light bulb moment

So rewind just a little, Christmas 2004 has just passed and I'm well into February 2005. Xtremewheels is busy, I'm still selling loads online and I'm still a washing machine engineer. Now one of the problems running the XtremeWheels business is that out of every ten bikes I sold, at least two bikes were getting damaged in transit between the wholesalers and the consumer.

It was only ever minor damage like a cracked plastic fairing, so I'd arrange to get the replacement parts shipped out asap. My wholesalers wouldn't pay for this, so I had to take on the cost myself which is really unfair, but the parcel carrier Parcelforce were the delivery company doing all the deliveries, so surely they would be liable for the damage. So I called Parcelforce, and they advised I could not make any claims for damage on these particular shipments because I didn't ship them, in other words they were not shipped on my account therefore the account holder would need to process any claims for damage.

So I called the wholesalers and told them they'd need to claim on my behalf, so they did. By February 2005 my suppliers were getting annoyed with all the claims they were chasing and they told me they would have to stop shipping my bikes to my customers. If I wanted to carry on buying from them, I'd need to collect them myself or arrange for my own account with Parcelforce, so I could process my own claims.

I was so annoyed, I was experiencing yet another hurdle in business. Just as everything is going so well, something goes wrong. It's like ice-skating up hill all the time. However, as time has passed and I dealt with this hurdle and many other hurdles after this, I have learnt that when things don't go to plan, I end up applying all my natural qualities and turning what was a bad situation into a better situation. This is an important point:

> *You'll notice a real entrepreneur will always see a new opportunity when a difficulty arises. If you think you're like this, then maybe you're more of an entrepreneur than you grant yourself.*

The opposite of this would be someone who always somehow finds a difficulty or a problem in a new idea, venture or opportunity. Anyway, here's how I overcame this new hurdle and turned it into a new opportunity.

I called Parcelforce in for a meeting. I basically said I needed a shipping account so I could arrange to have parcels picked up from two different locations every day, and taken to multiple destinations on a next day delivery. I was currently paying £25 to have this service from my wholesalers, they ship thousands a month, so they'll be getting better rates than I'm going to get. In my mind how can anyone send a parcel anywhere in the UK for under £25? I was expecting the Parcelforce account manager to say £45 or something, but based on the volumes I was sending he said £7.50.

Now most of you reading this might be doing the maths and thinking I've just negotiated an extra £17.50 margin – result! For me the light bulb had just switched on and I'll come onto where my thoughts were shortly. I quickly asked him: "Neil, if you can quote me £7.50 based on my current volumes of about fifty parcels a week, that's 2,600 parcels a year, how much would you charge me per parcel if I was shipping 52,000 parcels a year?" He looked at me bewildered and said "But you're not, Stephen, that's one thousand parcels a week." "I know," I said, "but what if I was? I'm just curious so I've got an idea of what the cost would be if I grew my company into a multi million pound business." He looked at his tariff, and came back to me with a quote less than £5.

At this stage I was getting excited, even though I hadn't got the rate I knew I was going to get it, well I was hoping for. I had this idea which I didn't share with Neil, but I asked him to give me the rate for a trial period of three months; guess what, he said no. I then asked him again and said: "Look, I've got this amazing idea and I feel confident I will be shipping a minimum of 1,000 parcels a week by the end of the third month." I could see his eyes changing as he was buying into me, but he said: "Sorry Steve, it's not as easy as that, an account of that size and on that tariff would need to be signed off by my boss." Ok fair enough.

The next day I called Neil and he said his boss said no. I asked to speak with her and I told her: "I've got this business idea which I am just about to launch, but I just can't get it off the ground using your rates of £7.50." I reiterated to her what I said to Neil, that I was very confident I would be shipping the volumes required to achieve their lower rates before the end of the third month. "If I don't hit target, you can just put my rates back up to £7.50." I would have said £20, but I didn't need to as she signed off the contract and I had this super low shipping rate. So, what was my plan?

> *Simply, to resell parcel delivery services but to make it easy for anybody to just book a collection online and have it delivered next day.*

I immediately got to work on a website and I called it Easy Parcels, and the site was live within twenty four hours. I had set up a Google Adwords account, but I wanted to do some trade on my first day so I went onto Ebay and just picked out about ten random Ebay sellers and messaged them telling them about Easy Parcels and how cost effective it was. On my very first day of business I sold five parcel deliveries, making a total profit of £10.25. I thought this was excellent. Whilst this was all going on, I had also agreed to sell Wheels to a Welshman for £2,000. By the end of March 2005, XtremeWheels didn't belong to me. I was so headstrong about Easy Parcels, that I knew this was the business that was going skyrocket and was my ticket to real success.

That particular day, the day when I had done my first five sales, which was also the day I had agreed to sell XtremeWheels, a close friend came round to see my other half. She noticed I was in a very good mood and asked me why I was in such a good mood. Now don't forget she was a close friend so she already knew I was a serial entrepreneur and thought of me as a bit of a Del Boy, but she also knew XtremeWheels was doing pretty well so when I told her I have just sold it for £2,000 and set up a new business called Easy Parcels, she was very surprised, and I think a little bit worried.

We lived in a big four bedroom house with double garage and driveway at this time and the mortgage was pretty big, so I had some decent sized overheads each month. When she realised that it was today that I had only just done my first day of trading and I had only made £10.25, she definitely thought I was mad and couldn't believe the pressure and risk I was putting myself under. For me, as I said before, this was a light bulb moment.

I knew this business had the potential of being a multi million pound business, I had so many ideas I had to write them all down so I didn't forget them.

I could see the business in my mind's eye five years ahead being a huge success, working out of swish offices, employing lots of staff. I felt the transition inside me go from wanting to earn lots of money to wanting to be successful. I wanted this company, my baby, to be successful - then you'll find the money becomes a byproduct.

But then something started to make me doubt myself. I knew this business could be huge, but I only had experience in setting up small businesses, so I asked my brother Sean if he'd be interested to come in 50/50 as a partner, but Sean was already high up the corporate ladder earning a good salary. Although I think I did a good job selling the idea to him, and offering half of the company, he said he couldn't take the temporary drop in money whilst we were both building the business.

Basically, I was scared, it's like I'm used to riding small baby rollercoasters but now I've just stepped onto my first huge rollercoaster, which is much bigger and much faster with bigger drops, twists and turns. I have no previous experience in setting up and running a multi million pound business, so why would I believe I could. I didn't want to sell my new dream short by setting it up and just running it like a lifestyle business like all the others. I didn't know of anybody who I could ask to get involved with me, someone with experience in the corporate world. So I turned to those CDs my mate sold to me a few years before hand, but this time I really took them seriously; in other words when Anthony Robbins said: "Stop the tape and write down your goals," I did.

I followed his instructions from start to finish. This was a new Steve Abel, I was up at the crack of dawn every morning trying to fit in my one hour of Robbins and mind exercises. I was applying NLP (Neuro Linguistic Programming) before breakfast, but then I found myself getting completely brain washed with it all and I was applying it throughout the whole day, whenever I got a spare five minutes. I didn't see it as a chore, I was very engaged with it all and I believed in it 100 per cent.

It definitely was a new me, but it did get embarrassing when my wife used to laugh at me as she was standing in the doorway when I was shouting out incantations and applying anchor moves to get me set up for the day. I'll talk more on anchor moves later, but book into one of my workshops or come and hear me speak and you'll see the anchor move in the flesh. I became so focused on being successful, this meant I had to sort out my fitness so I used to go spinning every morning down the gym. I remember where my thoughts were when I was spinning, I was constantly applying NLP and visualising my future with all of the great things I wanted to achieve.

By the way, that target I promised to achieve for Parcelforce, whereby I was to ship one thousand parcels a week by the end of month three, I smashed it in my second month, I had earned my stripes.

19:

The early days can be the hardest

I had to throw in the towel as a washing machine engineer, Easy Parcels was taking up all my time, even when I was only shipping fifty parcels a day, that was a busy day, but two hundred parcels a day with just a website and me, this is what my day was like. Up at 6.00am to do my NLP stuff during breakfast to set me up for the day, I tried to be at my computer by 6.30am to get started on any early morning same day bookings that had come in, then by 7.00am I'd be dealing with all the customer service enquiries that had come in from the night before; anything from failed collections, late deliveries to damaged parcels and just general sales questions like how long does it take for a parcel to get to Scotland.

I couldn't offer telephone support at this early stage of the business - it wasn't possible. Everything was done via email. My orders use to come in via email too in the first six months of business, so I had to sort out the emails which were live bookings, and customer service emails that needed responses. Back then I found that 80% of the bookings were done in the evening, where customers wanted collection the following day, this meant I could concentrate on the customer service emails throughout the day but keeping an eye on the sales as they came in.

Booking one order took a good five minutes. I didn't have the integrated automated systems I have now back then in 2005, I had to do it all manually by copying and pasting shipping data from an email to Parcelforce's online shipping system; grabbing the tracking number and updating my database my end and emailing the customer back with their confirmation and tracking details.

Although it was a personal service, it wasn't instant, though I had to make out to my customers it was instant to keep aligned with my competitors. The way I see it, it's not really a bad black lie if your intention is to implement what you're promising, it's just a little white lie to keep momentum in the business and retain the growth, which was required so I could reinvest profits towards the future development of the company. As soon as the customer service emails were up to speed, which was by about midday, I'd crack on and start booking collection orders that had already come in for the following day and deal with emails as and when they came in.

I'd also use the afternoons to try and work 'on' the business instead of working 'in' the business. I knew I needed a better website, one with a proper database that stored all the bookings instead of having them on emails. The payment pages needed improving, dealing with Paypal and other shopping cart software. But the real dream was to have all the bookings completely automated so when the customer booked the order on my website, the order would be instantly booked with the relevant carrier. All that came a little bit later in 2006, but it was important to have it all written down in my business plan so I knew what I was aiming for.

Until then, my family and I had to sacrifice going on holidays for two years, because you can't just walk away from this type of business if you haven't got the IT doing all the bookings and staff taking care of the customers. With previous businesses, I could just shut up shop for a week or two and come back to maybe two or three problems, but if I did that to Easy Parcels, it would be like leaving a baby to fend for itself for a week without food and milk.

By about 3pm you'd see a steady flow of bookings come in for the following day. The busiest times were between 8pm and midnight, and these still are the busiest hours when people like to book their shipments, but today it doesn't make any difference due to the systems I have, but back then I had to sit in front of my PC right through to 1am to get all the orders done.

Things did improve, and new automated systems were put in place, to the point where in 2008 the Crimson Business publication Growing Business, which did a write up on the business, commented: "His P4D business can process an unlimited number of parcel movements per day. In fact, so efficient is his technology, that a client could ship a million parcels to a million different addresses and Abel wouldn't even have to get out of bed."

I couldn't leave any bookings till the morning because I needed that time free for the customer service emails. Christmas was a very difficult time to get everything done, quantities would double, everyone is sending parcels. November through to mid December I was up at 6am and not back in bed until 3am. I was surviving on three to four hours sleep every night, I don't know how I did it, but I had to. I remember on a couple of occasions when I was really stressed because I didn't know how I was going to get it all done, I had worked out if I stop and eat the meal my wife had made for me, I was going to be in bed by 3.20am. If I don't stop and eat it, I'll be able to get to bed before 3am, but I needed to eat - so I used to ask her to feed me so my hands were still doing the work on the keyboard. This sounds crazy doesn't it, but it's true.

I was in a situation where I was actually needing the growth of the company to slow down whilst my web guy who I was outsourcing was sorting out the new site and some automated functions. But then came a really unhelpful development. Six months after the launch of Easy Parcels, the Easy Group wrote to me. Easy Group is owned by Stellios Haji-Ioannou, the guy behind Easy Jet. They wrote to me asking me to cease trading under the name of 'Easy'.

I couldn't believe it, I really didn't need this. I did some research and spoke to some legal people and it seemed Easy were just being awkward and they didn't really have a good case against me. However:

I looked at a recent case study of Easy Group versus Easy Pizza in a court battle. After a long legal dispute, the owner of Easy Pizza won and he could keep his name, but by the time they'd got this far, the company was financially broke and probably emotionally broke too.

I took my solicitor's advice and changed the name of my company and concentrated on more important things within the business instead of perusing a legal battle that I just didn't need. On a positive note, it was good this happened earlier on in the business and not four or five years down the line after I had ploughed tens of thousands of pounds into marketing.

Trying to find a new name was not easy. Parcel this, parcel that, I must have had about ten different names that I just couldn't decide on, but I eventually settled on Parcels 4 Delivery. After about 18 months, my customers were referring to us as P4D. I'd be looking around parcel courier forums and seeing positive (and negative) comments about this company called P4D and I thought, who are they? Oh it's me! So in my second year of business I rebranded the trading name to P4D, but we're still Parcels 4 Delivery and that's the name that's here to stay.

Around the third or fourth month, I just couldn't work at home during the day any longer. The sound of children in the background was very disruptive. Nipping out into the garden in all weathers to take important calls was getting tedious, so I asked my dad if I could use some spare desk space in his classroom/internet café on Orchard Way, Banbury. It was not a very nice area, but it was a lot quieter there compared to working at home. Although we worked separately, my dad was running a computer training school and had an internet café at the front of the building. Seriously that man can turn his hand to anything.

If you think I've done a lot, I've got nothing on him, he's been a salesman for a few companies when I was a baby, he's had his own driving school with BSM, he's been a professional photographer including glamour and weddings, he's had a chauffeuring business, the list goes on, but to top it all off, he's a reverend, yes a man of the cloth. I used to get stick at school because my dad had been everything and my mates' dads had stayed in the same job all their life. I suppose back then aged 13-14, I thought I was the odd one out so it's understandable that I thought my mates' dads were normal because it was my dad who was the odd one out. Hang on, let me think about that for a second.

Being an entrepreneur is being in control of your destiny, so the life you lead will be so much more fulfilling and adventurous than working in the same job all your life.

So ok, my dad was different, he didn't fit into the same mould as all my mates' fathers, but I think he's had the most fun and experiences too. I suppose it's no wonder why I am the way I am, I dare to be different, and different is scary to most people.

20: Learning to delegate

Now I can't go through and list every employee of P4D, but I will give them all a shout either at one end of this book, because to be honest without them all, I'd probably be even more successful. Not really! I'm only kidding, I only say this to get a reaction from them. Seriously though, I would not be where I am today if it wasn't for all my team and that includes the staff that have come and gone over the first 8 years.

I employed my first part time member of staff, Kerrie Clifton and she still works for the company today, full time as office manager. I brought Kerrie in to do all the data entry from 8.30am through to 1pm so I could concentrate on customer service emails. Although it was a weight off my shoulders, I still had to work through till 2am most nights, but this was because we were just getting busier. Until I could afford two nice desks, we used to sit side by side; and every now and then I use to take five minutes out and share my vision of the business and where I could see it this time next year. She'll also remember I use to show her pictures of the sports cars I wanted to buy, as the business became more successful.

Whether or not she was really interested, who knows, but she humoured me and I thank her for that. Kerrie had a picture of me where I had fallen asleep from sheer exhaustion by about midday. We think the picture was taken around July or August of 2006, but we can't seem to find it to show you in this book.

So the business was running smoothly and both Kerrie and I had our own roles and processes to carry out, but then one of my dad's side of the family died, and I had to go to the funeral. Not only that, I had been asked to play the organ for the service. (Did I mention I was a musician as well? A classically taught pianist, I also play the saxophone and the guitar - not all at the same time though.) Of course I happily accepted and it was an honour to have been asked.

However, on the business side of things, this was a huge inconvenience. The funeral was being held midweek, and it was in Liverpool which was three hours away. As far as I was concerned there was no way Kerrie could deal with the customer emails coming in. Only I can do that. But I had to delegate the role to her, which she was more than happy to do. Looking back I must have come across as quite patronising to her, but I think she understood that this was my baby and I didn't want her to drop it. I asked her to work a whole day too as I needed her to take care of bookings as well.

We left for Liverpool really early and I made my brother drive so I could be on the phone. It sounds really bad, but the only time my phone wasn't glued to my ear was when I was in the church sitting at the organ playing hymns. Even at the wake afterwards at a nearby hotel, I had to keep on disappearing into the car park to take calls. And before you think it was Kerrie on the other end of the phone, it wasn't, it was certain clients that had my number and needed to speak with me.

Later that evening when I got home, the first thing I did was flip open my laptop to see all of the sent messages that Kerrie had replied to. I won't lie, I was cringing at what I was about to see, but when I started seeing all of her responses and interaction with the customers it was like a huge weight had been lifted off my shoulders. Kerrie was better at this than me, not just a little better, but heaps better.

That was it, I had learnt to delegate. Another five years on from there, and I have successfully delegated every process in the business, to the point I no longer know how to operate some of our systems. It's hilarious actually, when I'm occasionally in the office and you get the occasional irate customer on the phone insisting to speak to the owner of the company. Sure I'll speak to anyone who asks for me if I'm available, but sometimes the customer will ask me to process the refund, or ask for their collection to be rescheduled for an alternative day, but I have no idea how to carry out either of those requests, not unless I grab the necessary process document, and then I have the fun of explaining this to the customer that they really didn't need to speak with me on this occasion, but hey, it's good to talk.

We worked from Orchard Way for about eighteen months. Kerrie eventually came on full time and I took on another part time member of staff. I was heavily driven by the thought of success and everything that comes with success. I'm going to explain more about my drivers later but somewhere around the time we were in Orchard Way, actually I can remember it was early December 2006 I experienced my first real "push".

So far all my drivers were "pulls", I was being pulled in a positive direction, I was creating images of success in my mind's eye that would pull me to succeed. So a push would be something negative that makes me determined to prove somebody wrong. I can't mention names or companies, but someone came to see me from a big named carrier company, this person was high up the corporate ladder. He came to see me because I asked my account manager to review my tariffs and because I was shipping increased volumes, but from multiple addresses whereas most accounts ship from one address - so a big cheese wanted to come and meet me. Now I was very proud of my business, therefore it was not difficult for me to sell my vision to everyone; I was so passionate about it. As far as I was concerned, this person was coming to meet me because I was an important client.

I prepared for the meeting and I was a little nervous, as this was the first big meeting since I had set the company up; I was probably having delusions of potential partnerships and I was worried what he would think about my tired offices. The meeting started off really well, and he got to find out everything about my business. When he left my offices I felt very confident that we'd be signing a new contract and strengthening our business relationship.

A week later I hadn't heard back from him and my account manager had no news for me. I kept chasing him every couple of days and when he finally called me back his attitude was quite different. He said my account had fourteen days' notice on it and advised me that my type of business was never going to be successful. He was quite patronising when he said: "You're a clever guy, you'll find something else." Well, I want to thank him for making me more determined to succeed. I now had a push as well as a pull to motivate me.

During 2007 I was looking around for new offices. We needed room to expand and I found some beautiful ground floor offices in a listed building on North Bar, Banbury. Having three of us in the front of an Internet café was getting a bit crowded, plus the business was also doing adequately well enough to take on a big lease. When I say adequately well enough, my year-end figures in 2007 were £1.2 million turnover, with projections for 2008 looking favorable.

The offices in North Bar comprised of four separate offices on the ground floor. The first floor was taken up by another company, which the landlord owned and on the top floor was an amazing boardroom, which was available for our use when needed. We started off with just Kerrie and me in one of the offices, and also a part time member of staff. After a few months we took on one of the other offices on the ground floor as I took on another full time member of staff. Over the course of the 5 years we were there, I ended up with all the down stairs offices plus I took over one of the larger offices on the first floor which was for me, and I kitted it out with very nice furniture, leather sofas, and fancy plants.

I think we ended up with eleven or twelve staff working out of North Bar, and it started getting very crowded again, but the real issue I had is that my team were all separated across different offices. We could all keep in touch over the phone, but in my mind's eye I wanted an open plan office with designated private offices divided by glass. So in 2011 I did exactly that, we now reside in a very swanky open plan office in the High Street of Banbury; it was a bare shell when I took the lease on, leaving me to have it all designed just the way we all wanted it which includes things like a sound proof double glazed partitioned office with P4D blue secrecy blinds inside the glass. All the team are in one place now, so staff moral has gone up. We've only been in the new offices for 17 months and our team is now 18 strong. We actually have more staff than desks, which sounds like it should be a concern, but it's working out just fine. Maybe a new desk structure should be on the cards soon, as I know we could fit twenty five staff in there comfortably, but currently they're all blessed with very large desks.

So I'm sure you can imagine I am immensely proud with what I have achieved. But I can't take all the glory as there is no way in hell I would have ever built a team this large by myself.

Here's why, and I think this is a very important part of my success.

In 2007 when we were starting to expand the team, the buck stopped with me to find that new member of staff. I got lucky with Kerrie, she could have ended up being an employee from hell. The part time staff I took on in 2006/2007 was a friend of Kerrie, so that all worked out well too, they used to work together at a previous company but she only needed a short term job otherwise I'd have taken her on full time. So I went to a recruitment agency and they sent me some applicants and I started the interviewing processes.

In 2005 when I employed Kerrie, she'll remember it wasn't really an interview, I just told her what I needed doing and gave her a few tests to see if she could do the job and that was it. None of these corporate interviewing procedures, not because I didn't want to do a professional interview, it was because I had never been interviewed and I didn't know where to start. I can officially say it was beginner's luck in 2005 because looking for that next full time member of staff was a very costly exercise, plus I didn't enjoy it. I was wasting too much of my time. When I eventually offered the job to somebody, I wasn't really feeling it and it was probably a decision based on a combination of pressure and not wanting to interview more applicants.

There was an extreme difference between Kerrie and the newbie, she was nice enough but needed constant watching. When my back was turned she was straight on her mobile phone texting. I knew before the week was out she was not going to be a benefit to the business therefore I had to let her go. A few days later, I bumped into the mother of an ex girlfriend I use to date when I was 16 and we got chatting. I mentioned I was looking for a new customer services administrator at work and she mentioned her other daughter, Petrina. The last time I saw Petrina, she was three or four years old and I used to bounce her on my knee. I still had this image that she was still four years old and of course she wouldn't be suitable for the position, nevertheless Petrina came in for the interview and she got the job. Looking back this could have ended badly, employing an ex girlfriend's sister, but on the contrary, although Petrina is not with the company anymore due to starting a family, she was a key player and still one of the most efficient workers I have employed.

My next member of staff I employed was a complete disaster, and ended very badly. I took it all very personally and it upset me to the point of tears. I then had a friend recommend a friend and it just so happened she had also previously worked with Kerrie too at her last job, and along came Amanda who is still with us today. It turned out that all the people I employed who had previously worked with Kerrie were perfect for the roles and I don't know how I didn't figure this one out ages ago. Kerrie use to work in the Vodafone customer service centre, which is just five miles down the road. As and when redundancies were being made, I was on the grapevine to cherry pick my staff. Think about it, Vodafone had already done all of the staff training for me so these employees didn't really have to change the way they were working when they came to P4D. I've had a few objective opinions over the years at the way I employ my staff, but hey, I don't think I've done too bad. I think we've had about five ex Vodafone staff in total working at P4D.

Amanda was the last member of staff I interviewed and employed; in 2009 my software developer, Chris and I decided to go into partnership and I transferred a percentage of company shares across to him. He brought along his father Colin with him who has many years of experience in managing people, which includes hiring and firing, so I delegated all of that to him, another weight off my shoulders.

I need to tell you a bit about Chris and Colin. In 2005 I instructed a web developer to design the very first Parcels 4 Delivery website, after Easy Parcels. The local web developer did all the design work but outsourced all of the clever, what I call 'geekery' stuff to a software company called Polyspaston based up in Richmond, Yorkshire of which Chris was the owner and director. Chris and I use to spend hours in email communication, which generally took place in the early hours of the morning; I can recall some nights where we'd be working together, testing stuff and the next thing you'd know the sun is up and you haven't even been to bed. Dedication eh! Later on I found out that he was five or six hours behind me as he spent a lot of time in Mexico, but he is known to be nocturnal too and work through the night to finish a project.

It wasn't for about year until we actually met, when Chris came to my office in Orchard Way (the first make-do office) for a meeting. I had the web developer guy, and some other people attend the meeting who I wanted to get involved with my vision. Chris was running late (as per usual) and I didn't realise he was bringing a young lad with him. I just assumed it was either his son or an apprentice. Now remember, I had never met Chris until now and I just assumed he was my age, about 30-35. He sounded like he was in his 30s on the phone, but when he turned up he was in his late 40s. The meeting continued and when it came round to me asking what Chris thought and ask for his input, the young lad, who looked like a young Harry Potter, started talking. I had to stop him and clarify who was Chris? All of us were quite taken back that this young chap was the brains behind all of the techie stuff. He was actually 21, but he looked like he was 14. The other guy who I thought was Chris was actually Colin. Chris was the guy who did all the techie work in Polyspaston whilst Colin was the guy behind the sales and relationships with clients, but I had never heard of Colin until that day.

So we all worked quite closely together on a contractual basis and in 2009 we went into partnership. I now had what I wanted right from the start, someone who I could pass some of the load on to. Someone who wanted to succeed just as much as me, so when 6pm arrived and there was still more work to be done, he'd crack on and get it done just as I would.

From this point we just grew stronger. Although we were increasing revenue each year, we had to identify areas where we were leaking money. Our expected calculated profits were somewhat different to what the actual margins were and it took a lot of time and new bespoke systems to be created to help us measure every part of the business. Today we are running like a lean mean machine. Hidden leaks are a thing of the past and if a leak appeared it wouldn't take long to discover it. This gives me tremendous peace of mind, when I'm dealing in millions of pounds of revenue every year.

21: Use your network to good effect

By 2011 I had structured the company in a way where all of the main jobs and processes were delegated to members of staff, but up to now I was still making the decisions on marketing and I was dealing with all the social media as well as being the main person who was responsible for new business accounts.

The social media aspect of the business is very time consuming and I'm no expert, so we recruited Natalie as our marketing manager. After about three or four months of Natalie working at P4D, she recognised that I was twiddling my thumbs with little to do, so she suggested I go networking.

With a little previous experience of networking my immediate response was no way! Years beforehand I was invited to a networking event where the entire room was full of pin stripe suits and no one spoke to me. It wasn't really my idea of fun. Nevertheless Natalie persuaded me to join a well-known national networking organisation to go out there and spread the P4D word. This time it was different, I had nothing to prove and I was just myself. I think it's easy to fall foul of pretending to be someone you're not, when you're in an intimidating situation, and that's why I think I felt uncomfortable years beforehand.

After attending regular meetings and when I say regular I mean three to four per week, but not just local meetings, I was travelling all over the country. The meetings would last two hours and would consist of thirty minutes free networking then you'd get 40-60 seconds to deliver your elevator pitch In front of the whole room whilst everybody eats breakfast. Then there is a 20 minutes slot where somebody presents a talk on something interesting and the last half hour of the meeting would be meeting certain people in the room you'd like to meet.

Now getting up at 5am in the morning to get to a breakfast meeting doesn't sound like fun, so I said to myself if I'm going to do this, I'm going to make damn sure my elevator pitch is memorable. You find most of the people in the room are so nervous about their own elevator pitch, they're not receptive to others in the room. I do believe I have mastered this; I have spent time and money with public speaking coaches just to get my forty seconds pitch perfected. It's not about using the same words every time but about presenting your self in a way that everyone finds engaging but without being a clown who no one takes seriously.

I also find, and this is a huge tip to all, 'sell less to sell more'. What does this mean? You see other businesses stand up and they get their 60 seconds slot to tell the other 40 people in the room what it is their business does. It's like a race, they have to speak as clearly but as fast as they possibly can to get all the information out there about their company. It's too much, and then when you consider everyone else is doing the exact same, most of the people in the room switch off. What I do, is instead of telling people in the room about what my company does, I try to speak from a customer's perspective; to tell a story which promotes my business, for instance....

I received a phone call last week from a lady who stumbled across my website. She has a business selling children's toys, from Matchbox cars to big Scalextric sets. For the past year she has been driving to the Post Office and carrying anything from one or two parcels up to 15 parcels from her car to the Post Office every day. Not only that, she has been paying premium prices for the service. Now, she is booking her parcels online with P4D and saving heaps of money, but what's more, the parcels are now being collected from her front doorstep. If you send parcels or more importantly if anyone in your network sends parcels, businesses and individuals, tell them about www.p4d.co.uk or speak to me.

Now that takes about 15-20 seconds to say, but using pauses and making the story dramatic, (remember how the story readers used to read us books on Jackanory when we were kids?) you'll have the audience engaged. Plus, I've used an example which most people can relate to, instead of just listing off what my company does.

A better example would be an accountant. How does an accountant engage with an audience? Not an easy task, but actually it is, but most of the accountants I see get their elevator pitch completely messed up. Instead of telling us all that you do bookkeeping, tax returns, VAT, blah blah blah, after six seconds of hearing this, you've already switched off. Tell us a story about an interesting client. You must have a client who has an unusual business. Spend most of your 60 seconds telling the room about this funny story you have, and you'll have them completely engaged and ready for the actual sales pitch. Something like a client who sells naughty lingerie that you had to visit, but apart from all the embarrassment and having to explain to your wife or husband why you have free samples of something in your car, you ended up saving your client thousands of pounds on their tax bill. All of a sudden you're the accountant with the sense of humour and the accountant who people want to refer business to. Seriously, work on your elevator pitch keeping this in mind, but don't take it too far and be a clown.

Where did I get to? That's right, I'm out networking four times a week. When you do this, you get to know people and you end up chatting. The more you get to know someone, the more likely you're going to refer business his or her way. You wouldn't refer someone you know and trust to someone you don't know and trust would you? I'm known for many things, but two of them are: wearing my heart on my sleeve, and being an open book. They both have their downsides, but in my experience there are plus sides too, which outweigh the downsides. If you didn't know me, but met me for the first time and knew nothing about me, we'd end up having a conversation, me being me, I'd try and control that conversation and relax you as much as I possibly can and I do this by asking you questions about you and your business, but I like to focus more on you as a person to try and find out what makes you tick.

If anything I like to think of my conversation skills when business networking being exactly the same as if I was down the pub socialising with friends and meeting new people. If you talk about work too much, you're going to alienate people. The good thing about this approach is that I don't have to try. It's just natural, and I'm enjoying myself. The work aspect can come later. If I just talk about work and it becomes evidently clear my business and their business are not compatible, then they're going to avoid me at future networking events, but if I just get to know someone as a person and we like each other, then we're both making it easy for ourselves to refer business to each other and we won't avoid each other at future networking functions.

I've done it again, I've got side tracked. So when I started networking, people would find out more about me and would take an interest in my past life as a serial entrepreneur, so I had to divulge into some of my stories as a Del Boy businessman and how I adapted my mindset to then take my current company into a multi million pound success. Before I knew it, I was being asked to visit a school to inspire the pupils: I was being encouraged to be the keynote speaker at many networking events whereby I'd speak for anything from fifteen minutes to half an hour.

22:

Dare to dream and it might just happen

Now, if I told you I was sceptical about standing up and speaking, would you believe me? Ok, I am a confident man and love attention, but I had a bad experience back in 2008 through to 2009 which made me very aware of other people and how they feel about me. The truth is, I'm a thin skinned guy, it's easy to upset me. If for any reason I knew someone said they hated me or called me an explicit name because of who I am and what I do, it would upset me. I haven't got on to goal setting in this book yet, but 2008 was the year I achieved my final personal goal, a brand-new Aston Martin

Vantage V8 Roadster with six speed paddle shift in onyx black with seven spoke anthracite alloy wheels, red brake calipers, obsidian black and red leather interior with red stitching.

Now why have I gone into so much detail about the car? You need to read on to understand why; it's all to do with being specific about your goals. I could have just said an Aston Martin, but that would have left it to your imagination what it might have looked like. Specifically detailing the car before I ever saw it, let alone buying it, helped me visualise it better. I do this with everything. Do you want a £1 million turnover business? You could just tell yourself that's what you're going to work hard towards achieving, or you could do what I did and detail what a £1 million business would look like.

> *By visualising your target in great detail, it is so much more achievable; especially when you apply your bite size plans and goals towards achieving your main goal.*

So, I had many rewards and goals on my three year plan. The Aston Martin was the final one. I discussed it with my other half at the time, and she was very against me buying it. She knew that was what I was working so hard towards. We'd already moved to the big house in the countryside with a gated drive, that was on the three year plan too.

The business was snowballing, and the car came very quickly after we had moved. I was in a tough situation, if I didn't buy it I'd have resented her and if I did buy it, she'd have resented me. It was all because the house we were in needed work doing to it. The plan was to knock it down in about three or four years time and build the house of our dreams on the acre of land it sat on. So I can understand in her mind, the £100,000+ Aston Martin was not essential.

Looking back, I wish she could have given me the recognition and helped me celebrate. It was a lonely day catching the train to Birmingham to pick up my new car. Who was I kidding? Driving it back down the M40 very carefully, was an experience seeing cars in the outside lane slowing down to see who was in this new Aston Martin. I wanted to be enjoying it with someone. The car only had about seven miles on the clock when I picked it up.

For the Aston Martin geeks reading this, maybe you're questioning how can this be brand-new? To buy a new Aston martin, you have to order it to your specification and then wait over a year to have it hand built. It doesn't take a year to build, but there is a waiting list. When you order one, you are obliged to pay a 10% deposit and then pay the balance a few weeks before the car is ready. You might not be surprised to hear that some people pay the 10% deposit when they order their car, but then after the year passes, their circumstances change and they can't afford the car. Aston Martin don't build cars just to put in their showrooms to hopefully sell. Each one is individually specified by a paying customer. If you see a brand-new one in a showroom, it's because of that, and it just so happened there was one available to the same spec I wanted, otherwise it would have been a long wait.

So I'm carefully driving down the M40, being very careful to not break the speed limit - not easy, believe me. The first place I wanted to go to was my mum and dad's house. No point in going home because I knew she wasn't interested, so that would have really got me down. This was it, I was going to drive the car up to my mum and dad's house, hand my dad the keys and offer to let him drive it. I couldn't wait to see the look on his face and hear him say wow, and express how proud he was.

I parked outside and walked to the door feeling quite nervous. The car was sat there looking amazing. I walked into the house and said hello and I couldn't keep myself contained. I held out the key and key fob which had the Aston Martin wings logo facing my dad and said: "Dad, I've done it. Come and see it and take it for a spin." Instead of jumping out of his chair and hurrying to the front door, he looked at me with great disappointment and said: "Son, I'm not interested. I don't like what you have become." He went on to say things about how I had all my priorities back to front and other stuff, which I didn't receive very well.

23: Mid-life crisis

Now if you're thinking, did I take the car back? No I didn't, I basically turned in to an absolute asshole. I was very angry at life and I ended up separating and was divorced by 2010. The divorce took a long time, but I was fortunate to have kept my business and even more fortunate to have a team around me in the business who had to step up and take the reigns and lead the company for around two years, most of 2009 and 2010 whilst I was trying to get my head sorted out. I can't remember the dates specifically, but it was a good year while I was busy living with a chip on my shoulder, but on the exterior It seemed I was living the high life, renting a swanky apartment, driving into London most weekends for the nightlife.

I was basically 34-35 years old, and having a mid life crisis. I was angry at Anthony Robbins, he was the one who told me to put this three year bite size plan together to achieve success. Well I did it and life was pants. I think I thought to myself, if I'm rich and successful, well then everything else will click into place and my family and friends will love me. Boy I was wrong, it was the complete opposite. I actually bought a front row ticket for a four day event in New York to see Anthony Robbins in February 2009 because I was so angry with him. I didn't get to speak with him personally, but he did touch on some stuff that I could relate to and I wasn't the only one there who had a similar story whereby they had followed his plan and succeeded but then lost their marriages. It seemed I was only focused on the success of the business and I didn't really listen to Robbins when he spoke about relationships on the CDs.

My dad was right. He wasn't jealous, he had watched me for the past two to three years become so consumed with my business, that everything else didn't matter to me. I was forgetting birthdays, anniversaries, or just forgetting to call to see how people were in the family. I had got to the stage where I was being judged wherever I went. Driving around in an Aston Martin has that effect. I can't mention names, but a very close friend told me a friend of theirs, who I didn't really know that well, said: "Your mate Steve must be a right bastard. To achieve what he has achieved in such a short space of time, he must have trodden on a few people to get there, so he must be a bastard." Now, that was someone who didn't even know me.

My friend apparently put them straight, he's known me for years and knows the real me and I think he understood I was kicking back at the world for a bit. I'm glad he shared that with me though, because a few things like that plus the relationship I had with my dad were really getting to me. Until one day when my dad wanted to talk, he knew I was struggling with it all deep down and wanted to help. I don't want to go into what was said, but we kissed and made up. The divorce was under way and things like the Aston Martin had to go, so I sold it to an 18 year old boy who hadn't even passed his driving test.

That's another story, which is quite fascinating. Literally two days after I got rid of the Aston Martin, I met an amazing woman who is a huge inspiration to me. We've been together now for just over three years, and living together for two years. All looking good so far, watch this space.

Now I got seriously side tracked there. Why did I tell you all this? Well if you were to flick back quite a few pages, I said *"I was being encouraged to be the keynote speaker at many networking events whereby I'd speak for anything from fifteen minutes to half an hour. Now if I told you I was sceptical of doing this, would you believe me? Ok, I am a confident man and love attention, but I had a bad experience back in 2008 through to 2009 which made me very aware of other people and how they feel about me."*

So now can you see why I didn't want to stand up in front of crowds of people and shove my success in their face? I had learnt the hard way; I know I'm a better man for it today but I did fear that people would perceive me in a negative way, similar to how they did when I was kicking back at the world in 2009. Not only that, I was a little ashamed of my Del Boy past. I was led to believe it was nothing to brag about being a wheeler and dealer when I was actually wheeling and dealing. It's a bit like, if you drive Rolls Royce, you don't want to tell people your other car is a Robin Reliant because it'll ruin the illusion. Silly thinking, I know. Maybe it's me thinking that I am very proud of my achievements and I don't want to dwell on the past. I want to move in a positive direction therefore I'd rather talk about my aspirations for the future.

Hey, I've just received a comment from my dad as I'm writing this book.

"A negative thinker sees a difficulty in every opportunity. A positive thinker sees an opportunity in every difficulty."

Great thought, and very true!

24: Selling the Aston

I wasn't sure whether or not to include this story, but on balance I certainly learnt a lesson here. I'm not sure how I'm going to put it to use, but it was an eye opener nevertheless. All good things have to come to an end. No I don't mean that, and I say it with a grin on my face.

I was entering a new chapter in my life and the car had to go. I had been separated almost a year, living out of a swanky bachelor pad which was a stones throw from my office. After a year of having a mid life crisis it was time to face my demons and get my divorce underway. I had to get rid of the Aston Martin, it was almost two years old now anyway so it was about time for a change. I ended up at a Volkswagen dealer near Oxford. I took my friend Neil with me. I called him that morning and said: "Fancy coming to buy a new car with me mate?" We parked up the Aston Martin right outside the Volkswagen showroom window, it certainly had the right effect and it got the attention of the sales people. Me being me, and wearing my heart on my sleeve I answered their first question. "Why are you looking to buy a VW when you have an Aston Martin?" So I explained about my predicament and the need to down size. I ended up buying a very nice, brand-new top of the range Golf with all the toys.

Meanwhile I decided to sell my Aston Martin privately, as the trade in value was not very good. I had a few calls and I had to sort out the time wasters from the genuine potential buyers. This one guy seemed to be a complete dreamer, but insisted to come and have a look. These two guys arrived at my office in a black Audi Q5, they didn't look a year older than eighteen, this made me angry as I knew this was going to be a complete waste of time. They were both wearing very expensive clothes, one looked European and the other Middle Eastern. The number plates on their Audi looked Arabic.

It was the European young man who was interested in my car, so I showed him around it and asked if he had any insurance to drive it and he replied "No, I don't even have a licence, I haven't passed my test yet." This really wound me up, and I don't know how I kept it together as I had better things to be doing with my time than showing two kids around my car. I said: "OK, jump in the passenger seat and we'll take it for a quick spin."

I literally just took it for a two mile round the block journey, and when we got back to my office car park, he said: "I'll take it!" I said "Pardon" and then politely pointed out that he was rather young, and had not even passed his test. How could he afford such a vehicle? We stepped into my office and he made a phone call to his dad who lived in Monaco, he put his father on the phone to me, who explained he was buying this for his son. I found myself trying to convince this man on the phone to not buy my car for his son. I said in so many words, and as respectfully as I could, that this car is a very powerful car and your son will kill himself in it. I also reminded him that his son had not passed his driving test yet. The father replied: "It's OK, my son is used to driving my cars when he is at home with me in Monaco." The money was wired to me within 24 hours. The following day, the young man came back to collect the car, but I had to drive it to his apartment in Knightsbridge, London as he was not legally allowed to drive it. This gave me the opportunity to get to know him a little, so I asked him straight up: "What's your deal then?" It turned out his dad owned a hedge fund company in London, so £70,000 on a car for his son was like small change to most of us.

I found it funny that he wouldn't just go and buy a brand-new one for around £110,000, but he went on to explain that his dad drew the line - it had to be a second hand car, after all it's just a runabout car whilst I'm in London studying. Gob-smacked comes to mind! My mouth must have been half opened with amazement whilst I was hearing this as I was driving south towards London. I had no problem with this guy at all, he didn't look down his nose at me, he didn't come across as obnoxious, this is all he knows, he was born into extreme wealth. I did want to make him aware of the value of this Aston Martin his dad had just bought; so I went on to explain how I had spent the last few years working my nuts off to be able to buy this car and then he came along without a care in the world to buy it, as if it was a cheap second hand stereo system.

I probably made him feel uncomfortable, but that wasn't my intention. I just wanted him to know what that car meant to me. The next bit is irrelevant but I may as well finish the story. We got into Knightsbridge and he navigated me to his apartment block just behind Harrods. He opened the garage doors using his key fob and I drove the car, what seemed like hundreds of feet under ground to a private residential car park underneath his apartment block. Wow! The Aston Martin was going to fit in just nicely down there alongside many Bentleys, Ferraris, Maseratis and I even saw a Pagani Zonda down there.

I parked the Aston up and we both headed for the elevator. We got to his floor and headed towards his apartment so we could complete the paperwork and then I'd catch the train home. The walk along the hallway towards his apartment was like an exclusive five star hotel. We entered his apartment and I think I was expecting a pokey one bedroom flat, after all he's a student. This apartment was huge and probably had a similar square footage to a five bedroom house. The views of London were breathtaking. I did cheekily ask what this was setting him back each month, he wasn't sure as his dad was paying for it, but he thought it was something like £12,000 a month. Then to top it off his girlfriend walked in who was picture perfect, she was only Miss Estonia 2006. This young man has everything and now he has my car...Grrrr.

About two months later I had a phone call from him saying he had passed his test and he wanted a quick lesson on how to use the steering wheel paddle gearbox, hilarious! Oh and if you're interested, his insurance premium was similar to what he paid for the car. It just goes to show, there is a lot of money out there. If you think of money and business as a big ocean, there's lots of it.

You choose if you want to go to the ocean with either a spoon or a bucket or in some cases, some of us take a great big tanker. Either way, the ocean doesn't care, so choose your spoon, bucket or tanker wisely.

25: Time to spread the word

I started to travel all around the UK speaking at many events, talking to schools, Young Enterprise and networking events. It wasn't long before an agency asked me to sign up with them and charge between £3,500 to £5,000 for an event. This initially excited me, not because it was me making more money, but because a value had been put on me for an hour of my time. Hey great work....if you can get it! But as soon as you make the transition from being a free speaker to a paid speaker, you don't get as many speaking opportunities because not everyone has that kind of budget for a speaker.

Now looking back over those 18 months, I wasn't doing anything directly for P4D, however there were many P4D sales leads flying in on the back end of my talks about entrepreneurship. It was indirect marketing. Lets face it, you're not going to fill a room with people if the subject is "Ten top tips on sending your parcels" but you will fill a room if the speaker is a successful serial entrepreneur who has built a multi million pound business from scratch in his living room - with over 20 years' experience of being in business and nine companies in total since he left school.

Well now you have an audience! An audience who wants to learn and pick things up from me that they might find interesting and useful in their own business. At the end of a talk, there is usually 10 minutes of Q&A's and you can always bet someone will ask what my current company is called and what's so amazing about it, which naturally leads me to a quick elevator pitch for P4D, by which time the audience want to hear my answer. They want to know what my company is, I'm not having to force a sales pitch at them.

For seven years from when P4D launched, we never had a sales team, it was just me. I was networking and speaking and then trying to keep up to speed with all the sales leads that were coming in. That's not possible, sales leads were falling through the cracks and I was missing out on lots of business opportunities, plus networking and speaking is tiring work, by the time you get to the office, you're not in the right frame of mind to be selling and closing business deals, plus I was at this milestone again where I was doing too much and I had to remind myself that I set out to build P4D up in a way where I would delegate the rolls and processes I didn't enjoy. So we recruited Rob, our very first sales administrator; a graduate with an appetite to win new business. We now have a designated area in the office for our sales and marketing department.

So going back to my previous point, I decided to knock paid speaking on the head and focus on free speaking events. I'll still take paid ones too though ;-). It's not difficult to get three speaking engagements a week and you can be sure P4D will pick up business from it.

After about 18 months of networking, and being a keynote speaker at most of the events I attended, I discovered that I wasn't really managing my business anymore. Don't misunderstand me, I have my finger on the pulse, I have full visibility of how well the business is doing. Every morning at 6am my system emails me a quick snapshot view of how the business is doing in the form of key performance indicators.

My business partner and I needed to regroup and have a discussion about the direction of the company and our key roles. Seeing as I was hardly ever in the office and I wasn't really managing or directing anyone, it only seemed appropriate for me to step down as managing director. All I can say is it wasn't an easy decision to make. Going back to my first experience of delegating a role as a customer service administrator, I'm now at the cross roads where I'm going to delegate the role of managing director to my business partner Chris.

Chris wasn't there at the start, he became a shareholder of the company four years after launch, so it was like handing over my baby. But if you remember how I felt when I realised Kerrie was better at customer service than me, and it was like a huge weight had been lifted off my shoulders, well the same happened again. After stepping down as MD and handing the reigns over to Chris, I walked out of the office that night feeling like I'd achieved what I set out to do. I still own the company, I still draw a salary from it. My title is founder and CEO, although that's just a fancy title. I still attend all important meetings. So right now I have what I set out to have; a "business". My definition of a business is a profitable company that runs without the owner. My girlfriend Roberta would jokingly tell you I'm retired, but the truth is, I no longer need to work. I choose to work, but I don't actually need to. I could take a year off and travel the world and my business would still be here. I'm not saying all this to gloat and try and impress you. As Robbins would say, I want to impress upon you.

So this brings me up to the current day. I'm in the middle of creating a brand identity for myself. I've written a book, you're reading it. I have ideas of a website, maybe future workshops and seminars plus I am mentoring a few people but I'm not pushing this as a business, mainly because it's free. I'm picking and choosing who I mentor. I get a kick out of seeing the results of businesses grow, especially if I had a hand in it along the way. You're probably thinking this all sounds cheesy, but I don't need to charge, and if I charged I probably wouldn't get the opportunity to help these businesses as they either can't afford a mentor or think they don't need one or they're too scared to ask. So I just offer my help and advice and it's usually gratefully received - after all it's coming from someone who has built a successful business, so they'd be daft to refuse.

Part Two

Introduction

Motivation from within

This is where it gets interesting - and if you are the sort of person who has read self-development books or listened to motivational CDs, then you'll be familiar with what I am going to share with you.

Please bear in mind what I am going to tell you is not just out of a text book, I did this myself and it works. I can't guarantee my methods will work for everyone, but I do know if you can find a way to get yourself into the right state of mind every day, then you'll have the same opportunity as me.

I said earlier in the book that I used to spend some time each morning listening to Anthony Robbins and applying his tools, but this was only after I had set up my parcel business. I know it was initially Easy Parcels, but to keep this simple I'm going to refer to it as P4D because that's what it's now called.

I'm not an NLP practitioner, so I'm not qualified to advise on any techniques – so don't simply go away and blindly do what I am going to share with you. Now I've made you sign the disclaimer, I'll continue.

Remember when I said I have a track record of setting up businesses, but to be fair they were all small lifestyle companies and then when I had my light bulb moment in 2005, I knew it could be something big, a business that could potentially be a multimillion pound business if it was in the right hands. I didn't believe in me, why would I? I have never had the experience of running a multi million pound business so why would I believe I could now?

I mentioned earlier in the book about the avenues I exhausted before I turned to some Anthony Robbins CDs. Instead of relaying tips and techniques straight from a Robbins CD, I'm going to explain it in the same way I do when I am speaking at an event, so I apologise to anybody who has seen me speak, and heard me say this before, but it's still worth reading as I'll try to go into more depth.

26: How to turn your rain to sunshine

On a scale of one to ten, one being bloody miserable and ten being ecstatically happy, what number are you right now? Don't worry, it's a rhetorical question. Can you also picture in your mind's eye what a number one looks like, it's when everything is too bad to carry on, you cannot get out of bed, you're burying your head in the sand and you're possibly considering suicide. Ok that's a bit extreme, but some readers might relate to this.

A number ten, the best picture I can describe and the one I want you to picture is the striker of your favorite football team bouncing down the field with joy after scoring a goal.

Generally speaking would you agree most of us wake up in the morning on a number five? We open up the curtains and the weather is awful. We allow the weather to dictate our mood for the day and put us at a number four, but if we open the curtains and it's sunny and the birds are singing, we allow that to dictate our mood to a number six. Do you think this is okay?

If you're reading this and thinking, well that's alright, as long as there are more sunny days than rainy cold days, then you're wrong.

HOW DARE YOU ALLOW THE WEATHER TO DICTATE YOUR MOOD FOR THE DAY.

This is one example of life taking control of you. The goal here is to take control of your life and have more of an influence on the outcome of your day, and then repeat it every day.

So, getting back to our scale of one to ten, you're at a number five and you're driving to work, waiting to see what the day is going to bring. You get a phone call, someone on the other end of the phone is giving you some really bad news, so bad you have dropped right down to a number two or three.

Do you notice how we allow it to affect the rest of our day, or the rest of our week? When you allow your life to dictate your

Mood-O-Meter

mood to this low level, you are in no fit state to be making decisions in your business, or even worse you're in no fit state to be making decisions ON your business. You're better off turning around and going home than going into the office and taking your miserable persona with you.

At the other end of the scale, you get that phone call in the morning on the way into work and it's a very uplifting call; you just got that promotion, you just won that contract or maybe you've just found out you're an uncle, aunty, grandfather or grandmother. Your number five on the scale has just shot up to a nine or a ten. You're feeling on top of the world. Do you notice how the rest of the day goes really well? Your mood will remain at a high level until life throws a curve ball at you, which brings you back down again.

Whilst you are operating at this high level, you may or may not be aware of it, but you are now in the best state to be working in and on your business. Because you are operating at a number seven, eight or nine you are automatically becoming a key person of influence. Your passion is coming through, you're glowing and people notice it. Keep this up and you'll be on fire. The problem is, it's not easy sustaining a high level on the scale because everything else in our life gets in the way and allows us to drop back below a five.

Now this NLP (Neuro Linguistic Programming) mind programming I do, I don't know if it's easier for men to do this, because apparently us men think and store our thoughts in boxes and women apparently think and store their thoughts in one big ball of wire where everything is connected to everything; but I'm sure we can all do this. So lets go back to our mind's eye and visualise all of our important thoughts, the good, the bad and the ugly. This is something the women will find easier than the men.

I'm no expert but I read somewhere a while back, the reason women can remember everything is because you can take an event and then connect it to an emotion, that then burns in your memory and you can remember it forever. Men can do it too, but quite frankly, we don't care hence why we're not very good at remembering everything, not unless it's got a strong emotion attached to it.

A classic example is that you all remember where you were, when the planes crashed into the twin towers in New York. Event, emotion, burned into your memory. So I closed my eyes and got all of my thoughts in front of me. Each thought has a little thumbnail picture, and they're all spread out like icons on my computer desktop. I'm now going to slowly start filing all of these thumbnail icons into two boxes. Keeping my eyes closed and using my hands, I'm taking all of the sad and unhappy thoughts and filing them in a little black box. This box is set down on the left hand side of my mind's eye. It's a very insignificant black box.

Now it's very important you don't forget about these sad thoughts, to be fair it's not really possible due to the event and emotion which burnt it into your memory in the first place, but secondly some of these sad memories have shaped and moulded you into the person you are today, plus loved ones who have passed away should be in this box too, that's if the thought gets you down.

I must stress, I'm not saying you should forget about the contents of this black box, you can open it whenever you like, but the rule is, don't open it at the same time as you open the gold box. And that brings me on to the gold box. All of the other memories and thoughts that you have not filed away in your black box should be happy and positive memories. Memories that when you think back to the day they happened, you can remember you were pushed above a six or a seven on your mood scale. You're going to file these great big happy thoughts into a big gold box. It doesn't need to be gold, it can be anything you want it to be, but something which is a million times more significant than the small black box. For me it's a big gold box with sparkly gems, similar to a pirate's treasure chest. I store this box on a shelf high up in the right hand corner of my mind's eye.

Now bear with me, you might be thinking this is all a bit fluffy, but you're probably already doing this. Actually I know you're already doing this, but you're doing it all wrong, and I'll make it all a bit clearer in the next paragraph.

Now wouldn't it be great if every morning we could take our gold box down from its shelf, crack open the lid and reflect on all of those successful memories, but reflect on them in the same way we did the day they happened? Why not? I said in the last paragraph you're already doing this, but you're doing it with the black box, but because you have not compartmentalised your sad and happy memories, you're confusing your happy memories with your sad memories.

If you can relate to the feeling of burying your head in the sand or feeling so low you can't get out of bed and this feeling carries on for days or weeks, then you've confirmed to yourself you are already giving your sad memories more significance than your happy memories.

You're cracking open the lid of the black box too much, which means your mood everyday is floating around the lower half of the scale, you're basically feeling sorry for yourself and you're in no fit state to start or grow a successful company.

27: How to think yourself stronger

Let's now tip the scales, we're going to force a new habit. For the next three months commit to spending five minutes every morning reflecting on your happy memories. The objective is to get yourself in the zone every morning before you start work. By forcing this everyday, you'll feel a little stupid. Why is it okay to lock yourself in a room and cry over your sad thoughts and memories, but for some reason it doesn't feel acceptable to lock yourself in a room and rejoice over your successes?

Be aware that, if you are the type or you know someone who gets depressed often, there'll always be someone there to offer a shoulder and encourage the negativity.

They may speak about putting your chin up and being positive, but it's still all got a negative tone around it. If, on the other hand, you're reflecting on all the happy stuff, no one's going to come and help you rejoice in your successes when you're revelling in it all; and if someone catches you rejoicing in your success, you might be accused of being self centered or gloating. It's just not deemed as socially acceptable hence why we're not comfortable with it. Unless of course you are lucky enough to have surrounded yourself with like minded people who "get it".

So every morning I used to force myself to open up my gold box and get myself into state. When I say state, I mean to reach a number ten on the mood scale. After three or four weeks of forcing something, it naturally becomes a habit. Without reminding myself I'd find myself every morning around 6.30am reflecting on my happy memories and thoughts and apply an anchor move too.

This is something Anthony Robbins taught me. Like I've already said, it's all a bit fluffy but I'm 100% convinced this is what made the difference and helped me drive my business to become a successful multi million pound business. The anchor move reinforces the exercise with physiology. Check my website for video footage of previous events I have been speaking at that have been recorded, or come and see me speak to see this anchor move, also known as the power move. It's similar to the Usain Bolt pose, but when my hands are stretched out, I spring them back in and clap my hands. Once the hands clap and pass each other, I've programmed my mind to celebrate, which pushes me straight to a ten on the mood scale.

Please don't stop reading, I'm worried I've already lost some of the readers, but don't forget this is all I did different when I set up my ninth company, P4D. The chances are P4D never would have become as successful as it did within the first two years if I had not applied these wacky and fluffy mind programming techniques.

So once my hands clap and pass each other I am instantly in the zone, and experiencing the effects of being at a number ten on the mood scale. Remember what I said about the football player? He doesn't just score and walk slowly back down the field, he runs and jumps back down the field punching the air, acknowledging his achievement.

It's the football manager's job to motivate the team before they walk out on pitch, and you'll probably find the striker motivates himself to a number seven or eight as he's running out on the pitch and maybe shouting affirmations of encouragement to himself to help get him into the right state of mind to believe he can score. This all sounds great, but in reality the state he gets himself into after he has scored is even better, he's now at a number ten. He has reinforced his beliefs and is now in the perfect state to score again.

The fact is we're all using anchors right now; we all have a song or two, that when it's played on the radio it takes us straight back to the emotional experience attached to an event. This is the reason many couples have their "song", it's probably because it was playing in the back ground the day they met, or when they first kissed. Every time thereafter when that song is played it just reinforces the anchor. We're doing this without even knowing about it.

The song *Black and Gold* by Sam Sparro, it's a great tune, but it was playing all the time at the back end of 2008. This was the year when my life was being turned upside down. No matter how hard I try, whenever this is played on the radio, my thoughts go straight there. When I met my current girlfriend, the song which was playing was *Meet Me Halfway* by the Black Eyed Peas - it was playing in the bar and it was on the radio the following day. Whenever either of us hear that tune, we say "It's our song", we get all mushy and remember the first time we met and our first date. This is proof that anchoring works - and we're all doing it.

So, why not create our own event and apply an anchor to it? This where we gather all our successful memories and get ourself into state, level ten and then apply an anchor move of our choice. Gradually bring yourself down from your level ten and then do it again. Eventually your brain will be able to recognise just the anchor instead of relying on you to gather your thoughts, to get you to a ten.

So if you can tap into that feeling every time you want to perform at your best, then maybe this power move is the answer. It's not a "fake it to make it" approach, I'm just mentally placing myself in the place I was when I was at a number ten. Using NLP to apply it all to an anchor or power move makes it easy to change your state quickly.

You'll know if it works because if you're like me and the hairs on the back of your neck raise when you're at a number ten, well this happens every time I apply my power move.

By the way, your power move can be anything, and an NLP practitioner will help you with this, but I use the Usain Bolt one just for a bit of fun when delivering talks, plus it's really dramatic and utilises a lot of physiology. This might sound a bit big headed, but I don't feel the need to do a power move everyday now. I wake up every morning to a 6am report on my iPhone, which gives me a quick summary of how successful my business was yesterday, and because it's doing so well I now have a pretty good momentum and start my day on an eight anyway.

Occasionally I might get fazed over something and I can feel my self-belief being threatened, this is the point when I apply an anchor move. Because this might happen in a meeting environment, or walking from my car to an office, the Usain Bolt power move probably isn't appropriate and I'd most likely end up being picked up by the police if I did it. So instead I have also applied my gold box to an anchor move where I consciously push the tip of my tongue behind my front upper teeth. I say 'consciously' because I can't be hitting a ten every time I'm subconsciously touching my front upper teeth with my tongue when I'm eating or talking.

When I consciously apply this anchor move, the hairs rise on the back of my neck instantly and it gives me a huge boost of confidence and self belief. If you have a load of positive, successful and amazing achievements that you are responsible for then you are really going to benefit from this technique. Don't question it, and remember what I said earlier, if you occasionally or frequently reflect on negative stuff like your depressing job or maybe you're in a pointless relationship which really gets you down and it's consuming your thoughts all the time, well then you're already doing this stuff.

If you don't change then I promise you you'll never attract anything positive. You'll just end up moving from relationship to relationship and job to job which doesn't give you that true fulfillment. And don't confuse positive things around you that have not been attracted by you. Be true to yourself. Define the difference between positive affects that LIFE has brought your way, (in other words luck) and positive affects that are a direct result of your actions.

28: Goal setting

At the same time I was motivating myself, and preparing myself to start this new business, which was going to be a multi million pound success, I had to put a business plan together.

Until this point, I had never put a business plan together for any of my previous companies, and to be honest it's not something I really wanted to do at the time. But now I've done it and looking back, it's so much easier to achieve your goals if you write it down and put a plan in place.

To make it more interesting, I did my business plan a little different to how most business plans are written. Well I'm assuming it's different to the conventional ones that the bank manager likes to see, but ask your self this question: think of something you want, ideally it has to be something that costs money. Now what motivates you more, being asked to do something and getting it as a reward at the end, or being shown the reward and promised it if you do the work required to achieve it?

Just to be clear, here's an example: let's take a holiday to the Maldives. It's a destination you want to go to, and you have a rough idea it's going to cost you maybe £5,000. Are you motivated enough to work really hard, to eventually go online or walk into the travel agents and book your Maldivian holiday once you've raised the money?

A lot of us operate like this, just that idea of getting away to that dream destination is enough to work for it and put the money aside so you can hopefully book it later in the year. I find it so much easier to achieve these treats if you actually spend time either online, or in the travel agent pricing up your holiday, looking at pictures in the brochure, getting as close as you possibly can to it to tease yourself but more importantly motivate yourself.

Maybe this, too, is a bad example as holiday brochures and websites like Expedia are easily accessible for us to price up dream holidays. OK, lets keep it simple, a child will tidy their room for the promise of a lollipop, or a child will be really motivated to tidy their room after you have physically shown them the lollipop which will be their reward if they tidy their room. Seeing is believing, and for me is a big key player with my motivation.

I am very visual when it comes to imagining and dreaming. I allow my imagination to run wild, I am the complete opposite to grounded and I hear people tell me frequently I'm living in cloud cuckoo land, but they're the ones who are apparently realistic, or in my opinion, negative. But I must reiterate, this fluffy stuff works for me. Dream it and then make it happen.

Back to the goal setting. I asked myself why am I doing this? What's the main reason for setting this company up and working my balls off? I'm 30 years old and although I now actually had this deep desire of making P4D a huge success, I still had personal goals and treats to reward myself with, so I decided to scrap the business plan and create a reward system, but then apply the business plan to the reward system - sounds like more fun straight away doesn't it? I call it my "Lollipop System'".

When we were children do you remember when our parents would ask us to do a chore? And if we carried out that chore responsibly we'd be rewarded with a tube of sweets or maybe a lollipop? Guess what, good news, this mindset is still with us and it's easy to tap into again. This is what I did. I got a pen and paper and wrote down in as simple words as possible, a list of the things I want. In this list were things like an Aston Martin, a Sunseeker yacht, a big house in the countryside with a gated drive, a nice new four wheel drive BMW for the girls' mum to take them to school. I'm sure you get the picture, I was basically dreaming and coming up with a list of things I couldn't afford but wished I could. Now I had to take this a step further and get specific on what this actually looks like in money terms. The Aston Martin I really wanted was a V8 Vantage roadster, so I got all the detail on it and worked out I'd need around £100,000-£120,000 for a new one.

Earlier in the book you'll remember I talk about this car in extreme detail and I'll move on to why shortly, but for now I'm just throwing a shopping list together and working out how much money it's all going to cost. The BMW X5 for the wife is going to cost around £50,000. Now as for the house and the area we were hoping to move to we were looking at properties upwards of £500,000, so I got an idea of the monthly mortgage payments against that, the deposit required and buying costs such as the stamp duty that comes with a property of that value. Boy this list is looking expensive, but at least I'm getting an idea of what it all looks like and then I can figure out the kind of salary I'd need to fund this kind of lifestyle.

Excuse the pun, but the yacht completely blew this monthly figure out of the water. The kind of yacht I'd like would cost upwards of £2 million, then you have the crew and running costs of a yacht; so I decided to be realistic, (not negative) and place project Sunseeker in a separate reward system/goal plan for later in life. You've got to walk before you can run, in the same way you need to become a millionaire before you can start even looking at yachts. I strongly believe I will one day be the proud owner of a modest yacht. I have a proven system that tells me so.

So imagine I've now got this list and there's perhaps a dozen materialistic items on it, and I have costed each one. I now sort them in ascending order from priority to least priority. To be fair none of them are a priority, they're all self-indulgent things but it's strange how the list also fell into an ascending order of cheapest to dearest, but for one exception, the house was the most expensive but was more of a priority than the cars, but I wasn't treating the house as a £500,000 expense, I was looking at it as a £2,000+ plus per month mortgage plus the initial outlay for deposit and stamp duty.

So the Aston Martin was at the top of the tree, that was my ultimate goal, it was this that I thought about every day in great detail. I can still remember daydreaming about a house in the countryside with a gated drive; the kids playing in the garden as I'd drive my Aston Martin down the pebble drive, and I could hear the crunch as the tyres slowly rolled over the pebbles as I pulled up outside my house and park at an angle across from the BMW X5. This is how it was for me when I first set up P4D. The truth of it was I was hard up, I had debt coming out of my ears, I was driving an old red Rover 214 but that didn't stop me from dreaming.

Although I had these big rewards at the top of my plan, they were not going to be achieved in the next few months so I set them to be achieved within three years. I had also figured out, to be living in a £500,000 house, owning an Aston Martin and all the other expensive things that were on my list, I'd need to be earning a lot of money per month. I was also calculating in pensions, ISAs and savings I'd need to be paying into each month. I came up with a figure of £10,000 per month take home. If I was earning this, I knew I could afford the lifestyle I had listed. If you're thinking this sounds like a complete waste of time, think again. I'm not saying this is the best way to get rich or achieve your ambitions in life, but it's what I did and it's a lot better than doing nothing at all. Having personal goals and rewards is a great way to measure your own success on your own personal level.

So how the hell am I going to get to the stage where I am taking £10,000 per month out of my business plus all the tax that's associated with it? So I asked myself the question, what does a business look like where the owner can take that kind of money out of it each month? I had to base this on my current situation, I knew what my unit costs were in the business and I knew what I was selling them for, so it wasn't hard to figure out what my margins were. Sorry, I'm not meaning to sound patronising, but I want to keep this as simple as possible so everyone can understand.

I was only selling so many products and services in my first couple of weeks and although it was already showing healthy signs of growth, I was a million miles away from taking £10,000 a month out of the business, but using a calculator it took me seconds to figure out how many products and services I needed to sell per working day to be able to comfortably pay myself that figure. I had also worked out if I was selling this many products and services, the revenue in the business alone was going to be over one million pounds per year.

All sounds simple on paper doesn't it? I also had to bear in mind that if I was going to get that busy, I had to have the resources to deal with it, in other words how many staff would I need if I was selling over £1 million worth of products and services? I'd need an office which was not based at home, so I had to start figuring out what the business costs would look like if I was running a business doing a £1 million turnover. Keeping in mind that what I want is to take a £10,000 per month income, I'm now needing to aim even higher to achieve this so I can actually afford the running costs of a business doing between £1-1.5 million turnover.

29: Building your roadmap to success

There, I had it on paper, I knew exactly what I had to do, I had point A on one piece of paper and point B on the other. Point A is where I was right at that time. This was easy, I just had to be honest and write down how my life looked right now. What car am I driving? What's are my personal monthly expenses? How much debt am I in? Once you have point A and point B, it's like putting a pin in a map of the south of England and another pin in the map but in the north of England. All I had to do now is work out the route and construct a realistic path.

Seriously, even at this stage when you haven't joined point A and point B together, you'll start to get clarity and you'll get the temptation to just get on with it, but you must not finish the planning here, it's vital that you join point A and B together.

Keeping the reward system at the forefront of my planning, I constructed bite sized plans, which on paper I allowed three months to achieve each one. At the end of each one I wrote down one of my rewards, it had to be a reward that reflected the size of my company at that time. I remember this being quite tricky as all of the rewards I listed were all super expensive so I had to create cheaper ones, like a new mobile phone. I really wanted the new Motorola RAZR V3, it didn't actually cost much due to the contract needing renewing, but I made sure I attached this as a luxury in the form of a reward for the increased revenue I had achieved in the business - which was in line with the goal I had set myself for a particular bite sized chunk.

To be fair I was quite flexible with my rewards in the early stages, but I always made sure I'd reward myself something and acknowledge it as a reward, similar to how our parents did it when we were younger. Something funny, but some of the people who know me best have seen me reach my hand high in the air, then drop my hand down between my shoulder blades and pat myself on the back and shout out: "Well done!" I do this just for fun as it gets a few strange grins but my point is we shouldn't take luxuries and rewards for granted and you shouldn't lose sight of the fact you earned it. I think this helped me plod on and continue with my next bite size chunk. Someone once laughed and asked me: "Why are you patting yourself on the back Steve?" I'd reply: "Because no one else will!"

Was it luck or was it determination, my three month bite sized plans were being reached within two months. The whole three year plan was achieved in two years. I turned over £1.2 million in my second year of business. I completely smashed my targets. I wish I still had the business plan, it was all scribbled down on three sheets of A4 paper, it'd make a good piece of art on my office wall. It could have been worse, it could have been on the back of a fag packet, but I'm not a smoker so there was no fear of that. I remember my first reward being £50 spending money in a particular clothes shop, but I can't remember what I bought, probably a T-shirt. The last three rewards were the BMW X5, the big house in the countryside which sure enough had the gated drive, albeit the gates didn't work very well so they remained open all the time, but the property sat on almost an acre of land overlooking miles of countryside and my neighbour was Mr Cadbury himself, well the retired Mr Cadbury - but his son would fly in every now and then in his helicopter. Mr Cadbury drove a Bentley so I was pleased to have my Aston Martin very shortly after I moved into the village.

Listen to me, I sound pathetic, but this is what my life was all about back then; I was on fire, I felt unstoppable but if you remember when I talked about the Aston Martin earlier in the book, I came crashing back down to earth with a thump, and then I went through a phase in my life where I turned into a complete bastard.

I mentioned earlier in the book, I went to go and see Anthony Robbins live in New York for a four day event back in 2009. I didn't get to speak with him personally, but because I bought front row tickets I got to mingle with many millionaires, people who had similar stories to me whereby they had listened to the motivational CDs and applied the goal setting techniques.

There was this one gentleman who seemed to have lost his way and was attending the live seminar to give him a boost. We got chatting, and I think or hope I was able to help him. He had a much longer business plan than mine, whereas mine was three years but I smashed it in two years, his was ten years. Now I couldn't even conceive the idea of having a ten year plan, but I'm not saying don't do it, I'm just suggesting you work to your limits and don't bite off more than you can chew. I suppose I could have made my plan six or seven years, and placed the Sunseeker yacht at the top of the reward plan, but for me it just feels like too much.

After chatting with him and asking him questions about his business, it turned out he was hugely successful already but his own personal goal had not been met yet, and this is what is important. So after asking a few probing questions it turned out that he hadn't been keeping on top of his rewards and he had lost momentum, motivation and drive. Without going into any detail about him, he reinforced how important the reward system is and what I mean by this is, it is so easy to get caught up in your business.

> *Although you're measuring your success and you know you're supposed to be rewarding yourself with that thing on your list and acknowledging the reward for your hard work, it's easy to convince yourself that you don't need that treat and you can go another three months and double treat yourself then.*

But what if the next bite size chunk doesn't go to plan? What if three months turns up being five months? The bite sized plans need to be flexible, I was smashing my three month targets in two months, but I had to allow for the fact it may have gone the other way on the occasional month; and if I hadn't rewarded myself at the end of one bite sized plan, it might be six months away before I can take that breather, meaning a total of nine months without reward or acknowledgement of my hard work.

As I'm writing this, swimming the channel comes to mind. I'm a strong swimmer, I have no desire to swim the channel but I know I could do it if I had a boat beside me which I could grab onto every thirty minutes for a two minute breather. So if you told me I had to swim the channel and I could do it anyway I wanted as long as I did all the work, well that's what I'd do.

So I'll tell you what, you can set your own company up, make as much money as you want and you can do it any which way you like, as long as it's legal of course. Just get a reward system in place and stick to it. To reinforce this simple mind technique, find a child around nine years old and incentivise them to do something for you, i.e. wash your car, or help with the dishes. Okay, not just any child, they have to be a member of the family. Lets say you incentivise them with £2 spending money. It needs to be something that they'll jump at so you'll be the best judge of that. They then do the job and then you decided to change your mind and not reward them. Two weeks later ask them to do another job and offer an incentive, unless they're stupid, they'll think twice about doing that job for you.

The thing is, our minds still work like this - but it's on a subconscious level so we're not aware of it. Become aware of it, apply this theory consciously and you'll reap the rewards and become motivated with great momentum.

30: How committed are you?

Here's a great story I love to remind myself of occasionally. I actually refer to this story at a lot of events I speak at. I don't know if it's based on a true story and I don't know who came up with it, but it really gets me fired up and has a very strong message. More importantly, it's not abstract, in fact it really resonates with me, based on my own experiences of achieving success.

There was a young man who wanted to make a lot of money, so instead of just getting on with it, he decided to be smart and he went to see a guru. He said to the guru: "I want to be on the same level as you're on." So the guru said to him: "If you want to be on the same level as I'm on, I'll meet you tomorrow morning at the beach."

So the young man got there at 5am the next day, he was all ready to rock and roll. He was wearing a suit when he should have been wearing shorts. The old man grabbed his hand and said: "How bad do you want to be successful?" The young man replied: "Real bad." The guru then pointed towards the ocean and said: "Walk out into the water." So he walks out into the water and he gets waist deep. He's thinking this guy's crazy. The young man says: "I want to make money and you've got me out here swimming. I didn't ask to be a life guard, I want to make money!" The old man says: "Come out a little further." The water is now up to his chest and the young man says: "You're crazy, you might be making money but you're crazy. I'm heading back." The old man replied: "I thought you said you want to be successful?" "I do," he shouted back. "Well, walk a little further," the old man shouted in response. As the young man got closer to the guru, the guru placed his hand on the young man's head and held him down under the water. The young man was doing everything he could to keep his head above the water, he was scratching the old man's arm, trying to survive. Eventually, just before the young man passed out, the old man pulled him up. The guru said to him: "The day you want to be successful as badly as you want to breathe, then you will be successful!"

I don't know how many of you reading have asthma, but if you've ever had an asthma attack and you're wheezing and short of breath, the only thing you're trying to do is get some air. You don't care about any football game, you don't care about what's on TV, you don't care about anyone calling you, you don't care about some party. The only thing that you care about when you're trying to breathe is getting some fresh air. That's it! So when you get to the point where all you want to do is be successful as bad as you want to breathe, then you will be successful.

So here's the ugly truth. Be honest with yourself, a lot of you say you want to be successful, but do you want it that bad? Or do you just kind of want it?

Most of you don't want success as bad as you want to sleep! Some of you want to sleep more than you want success! Well, I'm here to tell you if you're going to be successful, you've got to be willing to give up sleep. You've got to be willing to work after two or three hours of sleep. If you want to be really successful, some days you might have to stay up three days in a row, because if you go to sleep you might miss the opportunity to be successful. That's how bad you have got to want it.

For the exact same reasons, you've got to want to be successful so badly, you might forget to eat. I mentioned earlier in the book that on some occasions I didn't have time to eat in the evenings and I'd get someone to feed me. But you should be so engaged with your dream and passion to be successful that you will occasionally forget to eat and you'll go the occasional night without sleep. Are you motivated yet?

31: Emotional intelligence

This is something I feel quite strongly about, and it was only in 2012 that I realised it was something I had already been applying. I was invited to attend a free morning workshop in Milton Keynes, held by Action Coach.

The coach, Emerson Patterson, gave a fantastic presentation about all around emotional intelligence. At the end of the presentation and over lunch, Emerson asked us all what our thoughts were and to share with the group what we had gained from the morning session. There were some really wonderful examples within the presentation whereby we could all see a direct result in using emotional intelligence in business, and a few of the delegates reflected on these examples and wanted to learn more about how they could apply emotional intelligence more in their business.

I didn't want to burst the coach's bubble and say I had learnt nothing new, but I was grateful for the three to four hour presentation as it cemented the knowledge I already had, I just didn't realise there was a name for it: emotional intelligence, or EQ for short. I was already applying this, but I had been previously been applying it subconsciously, whereas now I am conscious of it so I can now use it more to my advantage.

For me it's hard to explain how I apply EQ, I take it for granted and I think it's just a part of my natural make up. I've already said I wear my heart on my sleeve and I'm an open book. This must give of a vibe to new people I meet that I can be trusted and what I say and promise, I mean it. This can also have a negative affect though too, in other words if my partner asks me if her bum looks big in a particular dress? Well let's just say I've learnt to be a diplomat in certain areas of my life due to many dug holes by yours truly.

Here's an example of EQ that we can all relate to. You walk into an electrical store and you're looking to buy a new washing machine. The sales assistant walks over and asks if you would like any help. Because there is so much choice available and you're not sure which one to buy, you say yes you would like some help. The sales assistant is already half way there to making a successful sale, you're looking to buy one after all, and so if he or she messes this up, well they shouldn't be in sales.

But we all know what it's like to walk into a shop and be in the driving seat where you have to firstly get the attention of one of the four staff that are chatting in the corner with nothing to do, then when you're actually engaging with them, they have no knowledge of the products and all you get is "Er" and "Um" in response to your questions. On some occasions it's down to us to suggest to the sales assistant that maybe they should go and find someone who can help. By the time you eventually buy from the unhelpful sales assistant, (who you can tell would rather be elsewhere) you've got what you set out to achieve, but you weren't really pleased with the experience.

There are a number of reasons why a sales assistant can be like this, one could be because they're young and shy, but this would come across at the time. Another reason is basically because they are rude and they're in a job which is a means to an end, this type of person won't go far, not unless they're doing something they enjoy.

Going back to the helpful sales assistant, if he or she is emotionally intelligent, they will try to engage with you and will find it easy to talk about something different other than the washing machine you want to buy. The clever bit is for them to identify whether or not the customer is the sort of person who'd entertain this kind of thing.

Generally people like to socialise and also like to talk about themselves if the other person is taking an interest. I'd say maybe one in 20 don't fit into this category, and it's not always because they're a boring ignorant sod, it can just be because you haven't figured out a way to click with them. You just have to accept this and move on.

Some people take it too far and they end up putting the world to rights and the customer either forgets why the hell they came into the shop, or they eventually talk themselves out of buying, and even if they do buy, the boss won't be too pleased it took half a day to convert a sale. You have to get the balance right – and for some people, it just doesn't work.

Have you ever had a salesperson ask you: "How is your day going?" or "Have you been out shopping long this morning?" It can be really awkward, and it just doesn't come across as natural. However, if they have the gift, it comes across fine and you'll end up striking a rapport with the salesperson making it much easier for him or her to sell to you. If they're really good, you'll get into a state where you actually want to buy from them, even if they haven't got the product you want.

I remember twenty years ago applying "open sales questions" when I was selling. When I say open, I mean asking a question where the customer has to answer with something other than a yes or no; in other words, they have to talk to you. I learnt this from the sales course I attended when I was selling reconditioned televisions, and it felt awkward back then. My big mistake was because my main goal was trying to sell, and then I was applying the conversation techniques - whereas what I should have been doing and what naturally came to me after a short while, was focusing on customer relationships and then the sale comes easy. I have always been an outgoing person, and talking to complete strangers comes easy to me.

Get people to like you and remember you, then the business will take care of itself.

Now I've said all that, but I still go about things in a different way. I had learnt about open questioning, getting the customer to talk about themselves so they feel relaxed, but it just wasn't natural for me and it's vitally important that whatever you do has to be natural, you have to be YOU! So what I do, and you may laugh, but I talk about myself, well not literally about myself, but I'll do a lot of the talking. I've been like this since I was a child so it comes naturally. I just feel if I do most of the talking to begin with, this gives my potential client or customer time to relax and get to know me. If I am open with them, this is an invitation for them to be open with me, and I generally achieve trust quite early on. I'm not saying this is the way everybody should be doing it, based on comments from friends and family, I apparently talk too much.

I used to take this in a negative way and thought I needed to change. I've just adapted a little around friends and family so I try to take a back seat and observe and listen more than I talk – it's a good time to rest the mouth, too. When I am meeting new people though or networking, I'll make that first move to introduce myself, ask them who they are and what they do, and if they're shy or slightly introvert, then I'll take the stage and do the talking.

Don't get me wrong, I don't talk about me really, not unless they're asking. I generally have lots to talk about whether it is the weather, the traffic, or something I might know about their industry and I can get a good conversation going based on that. It all sounds a bit simple doesn't it, and I'm thinking you're probably thinking why am I explaining simple conversation skills to you? I see it all the time, very intelligent people, probably with high IQ's and far more intelligent than me, but when it comes to selling or striking a conversation with someone, it all seems like hard work and doesn't come naturally.

I'm not talking on behalf of all intelligent people, before I get a horde of hate mail. I'm just saying, from my experience good sales people who get paid big bucks have a high EQ and not necessarily a high IQ.

And hand in hand with emotional intelligence, is our ability to make an impression. This is so important, we ignore it at our peril. And, as I was drafting this book, a chance experience demonstrated clearly just how everyone, everywhere, is automatically forming an impression about us.

I had a meeting in the morning and I like to turn up in a clean car. I'll say now and get it out of the way, it's a Porsche, but as I explain in this book, it's important to have your rewards in business, otherwise what's the point?

Because I was working from home on the book, I was just in my joggers and a hoody sweatshirt – normally, you'd be hard pushed to find me in public in anything different than a suit or at least smart jeans and a shirt and jacket. So I grabbed my keys and drove to my nearest hand car wash. When I pulled up, there weren't any other cars being washed, but to be fair, it was really cold and it was late afternoon on a weekday so most people are at work. This gave me the opportunity to have a chat with the guys who worked there, they were all eastern European and five of them worked on the car.

It was a really cold day, we had a freeze the night before and you could see some of their cleaning troughs still with lumps of ice in them. I was standing at the side keeping my hands warm around a paper cup of coffee from the petrol station next door, and the main guy who seemed to be running the operation started talking to me.

Because I am a big guy and I was wearing jogging pants and a hooded sweatshirt, he automatically assumed I was either a footballer or rugby player. It's not the first time this has happened; it's a natural assumption that a young man wearing a hoody driving a nice car, must be a football player - there is no other profession that can pay enough to someone who wears jogging bottoms.

I let him down gently. It turned out that while I was in the petrol station buying my coffee, they had all started waging bets on what sport I played. I explained I was working from home today therefore I didn't need to wear a suit.

They were working in almost freezing temperatures. All they had for a shelter was a shipping container without any heating. I poked my head around the corner of the container door to see what it was like in there and it didn't look very inviting. They were obtaining their power for the pressure washer from the petrol station. I piped up and asked them:

"Do you have a heater in that container?" The young man looked back at me and laughed saying: "No, we don't get a heater. A bit different to what you're used to eh?" He carried on, saying: "I bet you have a lovely office with heating, and have women bringing you cups of tea every hour." I grinned back at him and said: "I wish." There was no point explaining what my office was like and telling him what I used to put up with when I used to be a washing machine engineer.

It made me think though, what life used to be like, starting early in the morning, working from my garage. In the winter I spent the first hour of the day thawing out the frozen pipes so I had a cold water feed to do test washes on the machines I was reconditioning.

I know only too well what it's like to work in conditions where you can't feel your fingers; my finger nails constantly had dirt lying underneath them no matter how hard I scrubbed them.

> *People tend to judge you on appearances, and there's nothing you can do about that – apart from be aware of it.*

32: The shoelaces analogy

I say it all the time when I am speaking at events - I am a naive entrepreneur. I think I have quite a child-like approach in business. I get all excited about what it is I am trying to achieve, and forget about everything else that's going on.

A child can be forgiven for this as they won't really incur serious consequences, however an adult in business will incur serious consequences if he remains blinkered and focuses on all the great stuff, while ignoring the important things like HMRC tax bills, the VAT man and anything else that can cast a gloomy outlook on your day. I am still this big kid who only focuses on the good stuff, but eventually I get cornered and I am forced to apply my attention to the boring stuff, because it's been left to the last minute and if I don't deal with it now I'll be in serious trouble.

This is how it always was up until about 2008, because it was only me responsible to do it and I couldn't afford the staff to take responsibility for it. I've now got people who deal with all my accounting, and everything else that I find boring. The last thing I want is a job or process that's going to take me away from what I enjoy. I need to be kept interested in what I am doing otherwise I'll be completely demotivated.

Before I was in this fortunate situation, I have to admit I did cast aside things like HMRC bills or anything else that was not contributing towards my goals, like I said I was a naive entrepreneur, like a child that is promised a great big present, but they'll need to walk a few miles to go and get it. The child will not think about the journey before they set off, they won't calculate the possibility that they might be crossing busy roads or that their shoelaces might come undone and they'll trip over and cut their leg open. All the child is thinking about is the present. If their laces do come undone and they trip over, they'll get back up, brush themselves off and continue their journey, maybe with a tear in their eye but they are so incentivised by the reward they are going to get at the other end.

All too often, us adults are too cautious. Because we've lived a little we know the risks ahead of us before we even start the journey, so despite the reward which we are promised, we end up talking our ourselves out of starting the journey altogether. We all need that child in us, to help us focus on what we want.

We need to be aware of the risks in business, but do not spend all of your time focusing on the risks, because you will end up achieving what you focus on. It comes down to the law of attraction; think it, but don't just think about it, focus on it and you'll get there. So if your thought and focus is upon failing, well then that's what you'll do, you'll fail. But if your focus is on things around success, well then you'll achieve it. If you don't achieve it, well then you didn't want it badly enough, or even though you set out to achieve success, you spent too much of your time worrying about failing.

To put failing into perspective, I don't just mean failing, you can use many examples which come under the umbrella of failing. One example would be, if you're spending too much time in your day thinking about how you're going to pay the bills? Or what's going to happen if you can't afford to pay that bill?, If this sounds like you, then you are focusing on failure. I'm not saying that you should completely forget about the bills, I'm saying your focus should be on your goals, and you should spend less time thinking about the risks, just like a child would. When you trip over your laces and fall over, just get back up again and brush yourself off - then continue with what you set out to achieve.

> *The Chinese philosopher Confucius said: "Our greatest glory is not in never falling, but rising every time we fall."*

Very true.

This is another story, which I mention occasionally when I am speaking at events. It's a lovely story with a powerful message, but I'm not sure if it's a true story or not.

A young unemployed man went to the job centre to apply for a job as a road sweeper. He had no qualifications and could not read or write, but his passion was bicycles, he loved tinkering with them. When he got to the job centre the lady behind the desk gave him an application form to fill in. He looked back at her and said "I'm sorry, I cannot read or write." The lady answered back: "I'm sorry then sir, you cannot apply for the job." The young man was really disappointed, and left the job centre without any hope.

On his way home, he saw a young boy fall off his bike as a result of the chain coming off. Being the nice chap he was, he offered his assistance, helping to get the chain back on and tweaking the bike to prevent it happening again; the boy was happily on his way again.

The young unemployed man carried on his journey home, and after a while he started seeing bits of broken bikes on the side of the road, so he started picking them up to take home with him to see what he could do in the way of salvaging anything for his own bike, as he couldn't afford new parts. Also along the way he found a skip with a few bikes thrown in there, so he collected what he could and took them home with him.

He loved tinkering with bikes so he really enjoyed refurbishing these old bicycles and giving them a second life. He started selling them to make a bit of money. He'd always find ways to get hold of tired bikes next to nothing and spend a couple of pounds to get them back in working order. After a few years it had got to the point where he was well known in the area for servicing bicycles and he had to take on a workshop. Not long after this he started selling brand-new bikes, he even designed his very own bikes, which he had made for him by a leading bike manufacturer.

Fifteen years later he had eventually got the business to a size where he had loads of staff and the operation was turning over millions of pounds a year. Who'd have thought it? At 35 years of age, he made the decision to sell up, it wasn't long until an offer over £100 million came in.

To finalise the sale he had to meet the buyer along with both of their solicitors. They were all sat at his boardroom table in his office when the solicitor pushed the legal document under his nose and asked him to carefully read and sign on the dotted line. He looked back at his solicitor and said: "I'm sorry, I cannot read or write." The room came to a deadly silence. After a long pause when everybody realised he wasn't joking, the buyer spoke up and said: "What? You can't read or write and you have managed to build a company like this? Wow!" One of the solicitors then said: "Imagine what you could have achieved if you could read and write." The man replied :"I'd have most likely ended up being a road sweeper."

I'd love it if this story was true, but I know there are similar cases like this which are true. It just goes to prove you don't need to be an academic to succeed in business, you just need focus, passion and drive. You can hire all the academic people you need once your business is off the ground.

33: New inspiration

Most of us have people we can think of who are inspirational, whether it be Martin Luther King, Mother Theresa or Nelson Mandela. These are all famous people, however some of us may have people who are a bit closer to home, like a local business person or a member of your family. As you've already gathered, I look to people like Anthony Robbins for motivation, to get me fired up and ready to tackle my challenges but when it comes to inspiration there's one particular person who really stands out and that's my girlfriend, Roberta.

We met in late 2009, we were just out with our friends having a quiet drink when we noticed each other across a crowded bar. I know it sounds a cliché, but it wasn't as cheesy as it sounds.

We soon got to know more about one another, and Roberta played down her job, and just told me she was in IT. It turned out she was the head of her department and had a massive team beneath her, and she was earning a significant salary for her age. Going by her appearance - tall and slim with long blonde hair and a bubbly personality – you might not have thought she was this successful. You see, I was judging her by her appearance.

I'm not making out she looked daft, on the contrary she clearly had her head screwed on. But for me, someone who has no corporate experience, I struggled with the idea of a younger person being in such a senior role – I thought they were all occupied by older, more stuffy people. In the first year of our relationship, she landed herself with an amazing job at BP taking her pay to a new level, which really excited her, and it was great to be a part of it and help her celebrate and acknowledge her achievements. I'm all too aware of what it's like when you're achieving a high level of success and there are those around you who aren't comfortable helping you celebrate and acknowledge it, making you feel bad for being successful.

When you're in this situation, it's difficult to continue to grow and achieve higher levels of success, as the encouragement isn't there. But I touched on it earlier in the book; these same people who aren't there for you when you're successful, are there for you when you're in the gutter and failing. Funny isn't it; there's a subliminal urge to encourage failure, we're not aware we're breeding it.

Now why would I find this inspirational? I meet people all the time who are earning six figure salaries, but what's different about Roberta is that she grew up in modest surroundings. As the youngest of four children, in a family headed by her hard-working blue collar father, she didn't exactly have an executive role model to follow, or grow up in an environment where business success was regularly celebrated. Unfortunately I never had the pleasure of meeting her father, as he passed away just before her 21st birthday, but she speaks very highly of him.

So how did she break the mould? All of the successful people I know have successful parents - or at least their parents have a similar positive attitude to life; therefore they have a bit of a role model, or they have someone that has a subliminal influence in their life. I just don't understand how she managed to completely break out and seek different horizons. I find this extremely inspiring, and although Roberta isn't ashamed of her background, she cringes when she's asked about where she grew up. I suppose I was the same though, I mentioned earlier on that I was ashamed of my Del Boy past, but now I'm actually very proud of where I've come from, and what I've done since I've left school.

I was at a networking event yesterday and someone told me entrepreneurs are born, you either start out as one, or you're not. I stopped him in his tracks and said: "You're wrong". I believe the first 16 years of your life play an important part and help decide the sort of person you'll end up being, but that's not all. So if you've got a mum and dad who are able bodied and have their health, but they are lazy, stay in bed till midday every day and opt to earn a living solely on benefits, well there's a good chance as children you'll end up with a similar attitude.

If on the other hand the parents have settled for a job doing the same thing day in and day out, but they're hard working, then this will be the influence impressed upon their children. I was lucky to have an entrepreneurial father, this has definitely had an influence on my life.

Anyway, although her new job was paying an awesome salary, after six months being there Roberta decided she wasn't entirely happy. It doesn't matter how much money you can earn, you need to be happy in what you are doing. By this time I knew almost everything about Roberta. Her portfolio was impressive; not only the experience she had gained, but the work she had done for several companies where she had directly impacted their growth and profits. I said to her: "If you can do this for other companies, well then you can do it for yourself," and suggested the salary she was taking home was peanuts based on what I thought she could be earning if she worked for herself.

She had already thought about this in the past, before she met me, but I'd like to think I gave her the nudge and support to take the leap. She hasn't looked back. For the three months she had to serve her notice, life was frustrating; she got her company set up but still had no suitable work to take on when she was free. Finally, and a week before Christmas, a senior contact from a previous company saw her updated profile on LinkedIn. Now the COO of another well-known blue chip company, this contact soon hired Roberta, with an immediate start.

She is now earning double what she was from her previous employer; and she is planning the next stage for her business, developing it into something much bigger. To do this she'll need to start employing staff and create a team that she can charge them out for twice as much as she's paying them. It shouldn't prove too difficult, as this is what she has been doing for the past several years, but instead of doing it for herself, she's been doing it for other companies.

My final thought. One of the main things we have in common is the drive and passion to succeed. Roberta hasn't gone out of her way to motivate herself like I have; I listened to Anthony Robbins who helped me get out of my comfort zone and take immediate action, whereas it just came naturally to Roberta to realise she has to have a vision, and work hard to achieve it. So when we started exchanging stories in the early days of our relationship, we both shared similar stories where we had both gone without sleep or gone without food because we were so engaged with what we were doing. It's great to have someone like this to bounce off every evening; she gets me, and I get her.

Notes

Notes

Notes

About the author

Born in suburban Britain, and brought up under the strict but loving care of his mother and his vicar father, Steve Abel seems to have been cut out for an entrepreneurial future from the beginning. He endured school while enjoying a succession of part time jobs, and really flourished when, with little need for encouragement, he set up his first business at the age of 17.

With a clear vision of where he wanted his life to go, Steve embraced hard work as he drove down several business paths in the search for success. From second hand TVs and washing machines, to trying his hand as a property investor and horse racing tipster, it was not until he spotted an opportunity to link the internet with a problem getting deliveries arranged, that he created a truly successful, sustainable business.

Steve's drive for success brought material wealth, and the chance to enjoy the trappings of success and drive the supercars he long dreamed of owning. There has been some personal cost, with divorce from his first wife; but he remains a committed family man, on close terms with his daughters.

With business success has come the opportunity to spend more time inspiring, helping and mentoring others, through sharing his story. Steve lives in Oxfordshire, not far from his family roots, in the town of Thame.

Printed in Great Britain
by Amazon

78590178R00140